PRAISE

MW01007707

"*What's Next?* is a great road map for finding the life we desire in our soul and for which God has uniquely gifted us. Sid gives us clarifying questions to help make the significant decisions about the direction and trajectory of our life, especially during difficult and uncertain periods we all go through."

—John Haddad, U.S. field director, Young Life Military Ministry
Colorado Springs, Colorado

"Sid challenges us to weave an eternal perspective into our daily lives—to be bold, to be brave, to ask ourselves the hard questions, and to pursue our purpose and meaning. This is a quick and rewarding read. Enjoy!"

—Colt McCoy, winningest quarterback in
University of Texas football, NFL veteran
Austin, Texas

"If you apply the words on the pages of this important book to your daily walk, you have a high potential for a meaningful transformation in your life. The author of *What's Next?* personifies these leadership qualities contained herein as much as any individual I have encountered. Small book, short read, huge impact."

—Michael Pinkston, superintendent,
The Christian School at Castle Hills
ACSI Texas State Representative, San Antonio, Texas

"This is a conflicted moment in our culture: living longer than any generation before us, most people finish their life before discovering what they should have known from the beginning. This book will allow you to ask the right questions, consider the right options, and set a course for your future that will result in a life engaged in things that really matter. The time you spend reading *What's Next?*—and engaging in the exercises found in it—will be invested with the promise of extraordinary returns!"

—**Bob Shank**, founder and CEO, The Master's Program
Tustin, California

"Young men fresh out of college are searching for direction in life. *What's Next?* asks the right questions for fulfilling your purpose and passions and ultimately discovering a life worth living along the journey."

—**Matt Carter**, lead pastor, Sagemont Church
Houston, Texas

WHAT'S

Find the Road to Your Success

NEXT?

Sid Walker

What's Next?
© 2021 by Sid Walker

This book is available at special discounts when purchased in quantity for use as premiums, promotions, fundraisers, or for educational use. For inquiries and details, contact the publisher at WalkerConsulting.org.

Published by Walker Consulting
Editing and Interior Design by My Writers' Connection
Cover Design by Genesis Kohler
Cover and Author Photo by Wes Walker

Paperback ISBN: 978-1-950714-15-5
Ebook ISBN: 978-1-950714-16-2

THE WALKER
CONSULTING
GROUP

Will and Wes
**Thanks for your example to many. May God
bless you as you continue growing in wisdom,
stature, and favor with God and man.**

**Keep up the great work as you move down
the road to your success!**

CONTENTS

INTRODUCTION

Two roads diverged in a wood, and I—
I took the one less traveled by,
And that has made all the difference.

—Robert Frost, "The Road Less Traveled"

I magine your life ten years from now.

What will you be doing? Where will you be living? How will you feel physically? Mentally?

Will you look in the mirror and wonder, *How in the world did I end up like this? Where did I go wrong?*

Or will you feel a sense of satisfaction or complete contentment with the condition and direction of your life?

What would you say if I told you that the choice between regret and satisfaction is up to you? *You* are the deciding factor. *Your choices*—whether deliberate or by default—and *your actions* or inactions have all accumulated to create the life you have now. More importantly, the choices and actions you make and take *today* set the course for your future.

Now, believe me: You're not alone if the results you see in the mirror don't feel like something you would ever deliberately choose. And truth be told, there are mitigating circumstances we experience simply because we live in a broken and hurting world—circumstances like cancer that seems to attack people at random, crime, the deceitful or careless actions of others, or a pandemic that throws the whole world into crisis mode.

I get that there are things that affect your life and mine—things over which we seem to have no control. So when I say you have a choice between a life of regret or satisfaction, please understand that **I'm not saying your life is your fault. What I am saying is that your life is your responsibility.**

The trouble is that all of us, yours truly included, have the tendency to shirk that responsibility from time to time. If you're like me, you may not even recall making some of the decisions that put you on your current trajectory. Maybe that's because you settled for the easy path or simply followed the crowd. Or maybe you do remember the choice because it was based on others' expectations or discouraging opinions. Perhaps the main motivation for your career choice or another major life decision was to avoid disappointing the people you love and respect. Regardless, it's often the default or "obvious" choices that push us along the path of least resistance—which often turns out to be a road we later regret taking.

Most people move along in life without really thinking about what's next. We act without ever making conscious choices or considering the direction we are headed. I know that was true for me early on. Humans tend to run on emotion and drift toward what feels good or easy. In the coaching and mentoring sessions I've conducted, one of the most common comments I hear is, "I just want to be happy."

Who doesn't? Everyone wants to be happy! But happiness is not the ultimate goal. Sure, it can be a side benefit of a life well lived, but it should not be the goal. Why? Because when your goal is happiness, you will never be fully satisfied.

Consider King Solomon, whose story is told in the Old Testament. He devoted his life to being happy. We even have him to thank for the phrase "eat, drink, and be merry." If we make happiness our goal, we may end up just like Solomon. After pursuing every pleasure, from food and wealth to women and entertainment, King Solomon reflected on his life and acknowledged that *everything* he had devoted his time and attention to attaining was meaningless.

I don't want to end up with a *meaningless* life. I am certain you don't either.

So if happiness isn't the goal, what is?

I believe the answer—the goal—will be different for each of us, but the way we find a goal that *is* worthy of pursuit is always the same: We have to ask the right questions.

Think about it: Have you ever stopped to ask, "What do I want out of life?" or better yet, "What really matters to me?" In this book, we'll explore questions that will help you make the kind of choices that lead to a life well lived. Questions that will help you find your way to, "What's next?"

Now if you're thinking, *I don't have time for this!*, let me caution you: Until you are willing to reflect on and answer a few hard questions, you will continue to wander aimlessly and follow the crowd down the path of least resistance. And ultimately, you will likely end up stuck in a life of regret that is void of meaning or purpose.

If you're anything like me, you want your life to count. You want your interactions and example to make a difference in the lives of the people you care about most. Years from now, you want to be able to look back with a sense of peace rather than regret. So I challenge you to make time for reflection. Give yourself thirty minutes a day or an hour one day a week to stop and think about one question from the chapters of this book. I promise you that the answers, and the actions you take as a result, will make a difference in your life. Some of the questions we'll consider include…

- Who am I?
- Why am I here?
- What do I want?
- What is my purpose?
- What does God expect of me?

One of the most important questions we'll consider is, *What really matters?* Personally, I am convinced that the most important thing in life, ranking even higher than family, work, or accomplishments, is a person's eternal destiny. Knowing where you are going when your time on earth is over—and whom you are taking with you—is even more important than knowing which school to attend, whom to marry, or which career moves to make. The short game always impacts the long game, which is why the topic of eternity is woven throughout the pages of this book.

My hope is that you'll uncover answers that put you on a path that leads to the kind of life and eternity you desire.

Many who have already gone before us have arrived at the end of their lives, only to realize it is too late to make changes. With regret, the question surfaces, "Why didn't I . . . ?" You don't want to be that guy!

Don't wait until it is too late. Start today. Be brave enough to ask the hard questions. Use your answers to make the choices and moves that will ensure the way you spend your life is *full* of meaning.

WHY ARE YOU HERE?

If you're bored with life—you don't get up every morning with a burning desire to do things—you don't have enough goals.

—Lou Holtz

From Day One, most parents simply want their children to be happy. Almost daily, children are asked questions to help ensure their happiness:

What do you want to do today?

What do want to wear?

What do you want to eat?

You're seeing the theme, right? It's always, *What do you want . . . ?* After all, we want our children to be happy. We love them. We want to see them smile. And let's be honest, the whole house is happier when the children are happy—or at least placated.

I'm not pointing fingers, here. My wife, Amy, and I have two boys. We wanted to make sure they ate well so they would grow up to be big, strong, young men. We tried to feed them healthy food, but our idea of healthy food and what our boys would actually eat didn't always match up. To meet somewhere close to the middle, we ended up making chicken strips and French fries our go-to meal for them. Chicken strips and fries were what they liked, it was what they asked for, and most importantly to us, it was what they would eat. In other words, we gave in to what they wanted. And like so many children do after getting what they want, they came to expect it. Chicken fingers and fries were on demand for just about any meal.

No wonder children think life is all about them. They grow up accustomed to the idea that their parents exist simply to make them happy! Unfortunately, but not intentionally, parents instill the mindset in their children that "it's all about me."

It's easy to hang on to that mentality even after childhood. Society continually reinforces the idea that happiness—defined as getting whatever you want, whenever you want it—is to be expected. Advertising messages constantly direct us toward the pursuit of happiness. If you play this sport, wear this brand, eat at this restaurant, drink this beverage, drive this car, and so on, you are guaranteed a life of pure happiness.

So, how's that working out?

Actually, it isn't working out at all. Research shows that Americans are less happy than ever before. We have more wealth, more access to information, more advanced technology and therefore we are more connected than any other time in history, and yet we are unhappier than the generations before us who grew up with far less. Take a look at these statistics:

- **People are dissatisfied at work.** According to a 2017 Gallop poll, almost 70 percent of US workers are not engaged at work, and more than 50 percent are watching for new opportunities.
- **Mental health issues are increasing.** In the United States, 19.1 percent of adults experienced mental illness in 2018. That number represents one out of every five adults. This decline in mental health includes issues ranging from an inability to focus and attention deficit/hyperactivity disorder (ADHD), to anxiety, bipolar disorders, depression, eating disorders, and more.
- **The suicide rate is rising.** The death rate by suicide in those aged 10–24 increased 57.4 percent between 2007–2018, which signals a growing mental health crisis in this nation and the need for change.

Jeffrey Sachs, a professor at Columbia University, blames unhappiness for an uptick in addictions, saying, "The compulsive pursuit of substance abuse and addictive behaviors is causing severe unhappiness." According to Sachs, a number of distressing trends plaguing the country stem from addictive behaviors, including opioid use, obesity, and depression.

Dissatisfaction and unhappiness are not new problems or recent discoveries. King David's son, Solomon, followed in his father's footsteps as King of Israel. In the

Old Testament and from other historic documents, we know that Solomon was considered the wisest man who had ever lived; he was also the wealthiest man of his time. Solomon denied himself nothing. He *literally* got whatever he wanted—from women to wealth—but he was never satisfied.

Near the end of his life, he wrote these depressingly reflective thoughts: "I hated my life, because the work that is done under the sun was grievous to me. All of it is meaningless, a chasing after the wind. I hated all things I had toiled for" (Ecclesiastes 2:17–18, NIV).

Solomon's lifelong pursuit was happiness, and in the end, he had none.

Can you imagine looking back on your life, hating everything you had traded your time, money, and energy for? How futile. How pitiful.

No one wants to end up that way.

And yet, so many people do.

We strive for happiness only to discover that happiness is in the moment. It does not last. We enjoy its elation for mere minutes (sometimes seconds) before another wish or worry comes along. And because happiness is fleeting, we have often become a society in pursuit of a constantly moving target, not unlike those videos of cats futilely chasing red laser dots.

Have you ever thought you'd be happy if you could . . .

- Get more likes on social media?
- Get a date with *that* person?
- Attend the right college?

- Land your dream job?
- Earn more money?
- Get your body in shape?
- Take that vacation?
- _____ (fill in the blank)?

There is nothing wrong with anything on that list, but if the outcome you are hoping to achieve by going after any one of those goals is happiness, you will never be satisfied. Even if you achieve the goal, it won't be enough to keep you happy. Yeah, you'll feel a momentary high, but before long, you'll need another hit. Happiness is fleeting, remember? The high it offers is always followed by a low.

Is it any wonder that depression and dissatisfaction are on the rise? We are chasing the wrong goals for the wrong reasons. We don't feel happy with what we have, and all the energy, money, and *life* we've given in exchange only to end up *un*happy feels like a huge waste. *Meaningless.*

Life, Liberty, and the Pursuit of Purpose

If happiness isn't as worthy a pursuit as we've been led to believe, what is? If you were not put here on earth to pursue happiness, then why are you here? What is it that is worth living for?

I can't give you the answers to those questions, or for that matter, to any of the questions in this book. What I can tell you is that I believe you were created for meaning and purpose. It is in that pursuit of your purpose that you will find lasting joy and contentment.

DESIRE IS THE STARTING POINT OF ALL ACHIEVEMENT, NOT A HOPE, NOT A WISH, BUT A KEEN PULSATING DESIRE WHICH TRANSCENDS EVERYTHING.

—NAPOLEON HILL, *THINK AND GROW RICH*

Although I can't tell you what your purpose is, I can tell you that the answer has to do with desire.

Trust in the Lord and do good;
dwell in the land and enjoy safe pasture.
Take delight in the Lord,
and he will give you the desires of your heart.
—David, Psalms 37:3–4 (NIV)

What drives you? What's your motivation? I believe we all have a God-given desire that pushes us toward our God-given purpose. You just have to find yours. I promise, it's within you. But you may have to dig for it. (In the next chapter, I'll share some of the tools that may help you in the excavation process.)

For some people, this desire surfaces easily. We all know people who, from an early age, knew exactly what they wanted to do when they grew up. My good friend Lance Jones is one of those people. He enjoyed math as a child and excelled at it in school. In college, he majored in accounting. After graduation, he earned his Certified Public Accountant's license, went to work for an accounting firm, is still with that same firm, and has loved every minute of his career! (Okay, perhaps not every minute of tax season. After all, nobody could love that, could they?) Lance identified his desire, used that desire to drive his education and career choices, and today he continues to enjoy his work.

Many people, myself included, aren't that lucky. For most of us, finding our driving desire is a process—perhaps even a lifelong journey filled with detours and U-turns. And yes, all that re-routing may seem meaningless, but it isn't.

While you are in the process of discovering what drives you, you can work and live with meaning and purpose by engaging in worthy causes, performing satisfactory work, setting productive personal and professional goals, and working towards those goals. And you can use the knowledge, experience, and insight from all of those experiences to answer the questions that help you determine *what's next* for you.

If you know your purpose and are on a positive path forward, great! This book will serve to reenergize you on your way. If, however, you are feeling lost or somewhat discouraged, please don't despair. As you engage in the process of reflection—of answering the hard questions—you'll find hope for your future and contentment in the journey.

> **Many are the plans in a person's heart,**
> **but it is the Lord's purpose that prevails.**
> **—Solomon, Proverbs 19:21 (NIV)**

My greatest hope for this process is that you will discover how to live with your greater purpose in mind. I believe we are all made for a bigger purpose. An eternal one.

God has placed in the heart of each of us a yearning to know Him. That desire—that purpose—will never completely be fulfilled until we come to know Him and live in His presence for eternity. But that doesn't mean we can't live today with our ultimate purpose in mind. We have a choice: You and I can live each day, completely focused on what *we* want. We can continue to live with the belief that life is all about us and our happiness. Or we can live with an eternal mindset that puts God and what He wants at the center. Jesus was once asked what was most important. He answered, loving God and loving people. If we choose to move toward our eternal purpose now, our focus and our actions will be on doing our best work, as if working for God, and loving others.

If you choose the path oriented by your greater purpose—your eternal purpose—you will be on your way to finding your life's purpose on earth as well.

You can have everything in life you want, if you will just help other people get what they want.
—Zig Ziglar

Now all has been heard; here is the conclusion of the matter: Fear God and keep his commandments, for this is the duty of all mankind.
—Solomon, Ecclesiastes 12:13 (NIV)

More Questions to Consider

❑ What gives you the most satisfaction? Not what makes you momentarily happy, but what provides a true sense of fulfillment?

❑ How often do you feel satisfied, fulfilled, and content?

❑ What are your natural strengths? What do you have a true talent or innate ability for?

❑ Are you currently using those strengths in your work or on a regular basis?

❑ What would it feel like if you could identify and use your individual strengths and find fulfillment every day or even on most days?

WHO ARE YOU?

For you created my inmost being; you knit me together in my mother's womb. I praise you because I am fearfully and wonderfully made.

—David, Psalm 139:13–14 (NIV)

Who are you? Do you know? Can you tell me right now what makes you a one-of-a-kind, limited edition?

If your answer starts with, *I, well, I uh . . . I'm just your average guy . . .* , you are not alone.

A few people are wired to know exactly who they are, but for the majority of us, it takes years, decades—even half our lives or more—to truly know who we are and what makes us unique. That was certainly true for me.

After serving as Vice President for Development at Stephen F. Austin State University, I went to work for a company owned by an SFA alumnus. The CEO of that company asked me one day, "Sid, what is the desire of your heart?"

The question caught me off guard, mostly because I had never stopped to genuinely consider what I wanted out of life or what I really wanted to do. Also, how do you answer that question when it's your boss asking? Shouldn't your desire be working for the company? *Awkward.* The fact that I was already past fifty years old and I still didn't know the answer added to my discomfort with the question.

What *did* I *really* want to do?

I was stumped.

Up to that point, I had always been a fly-by-the-seat-of-my-pants kind of person. Sure, I had set a few goals and followed through to completion, including earning a college degree, running a marathon, and becoming a certified SCUBA diver. But most of the things I had accomplished and decisions I had made were simply logical next steps or opportunities right in front of me. Other times, I simply followed along. That was certainly the case when I was younger.

Growing up, I often did what my friends were doing without really thinking about how it fit into any kind of plan. My best bud throughout high school and college was Mike Thomas, and we did everything together: We attended the same summer camp, raised animals for the county livestock show, and trapped varmints and sold their pelts to earn a little extra cash. We roomed together at the same college that our dads had both attended, chose the same major, and took some of the same classes at the same times. Those were all good things, and I have many great memories of those years, but I do not recall even once asking the question, "Is this what I really want to do?" I did

MAY HE GIVE YOU THE DESIRE OF YOUR HEART AND MAKE ALL YOUR PLANS SUCCEED.

—DAVID, PSALMS 20:4 (NIV)

whatever Mike was doing. I wonder now if he would say he did whatever I was doing. The point is, neither of us gave much thought at all to our choices. We did what sounded fun at the time. Maybe that's not *bad*; in fact, it's likely quite normal. But there was certainly nothing intentional about it.

Back to the question at hand: What was my heart's desire?

I had no idea.

Seeing that I was at a loss, the CEO recommended I take the DISC Personality Profile. Notice that she didn't ask me to make a list of things I like to do or to write down all of my hopes and dreams. Her suggestion wasn't about the *what*, it was about figuring out the *who*—me, myself, and I.

I took the Team Dimensions Profile 2.0 online assessment through DiscProfile.com. The results provided important insight and served as a timely reminder. My profile came back as that of "Advancer, tending toward Execution." My core characteristics included the following:

- Concerned with feelings and relationships
- Pays close attention to personal communication
- Tackles detailed projects with concrete results
- Creates energy and excitement, acts on instinct
- Brings groups together, networking
- Teaching, training, organizing

Reflecting on a few previous jobs that I had truly enjoyed, I realized those characteristics were the exact qualities that had enabled me to find contentment and success in my work. It didn't matter how varied the work was—a summer camp counselor, a math teacher and coach, a fundraiser for college-level teams—those traits came into play in a big way in several roles. Suddenly I could see the common threads: working with people, building relationships, teaching and training, and *getting stuff done*. Results, baby!

Even though I had passed the halfway point in my life on earth, gaining a true understanding of myself was a turning point. I finally had a clear picture of who I was. I had identified my core strengths and had begun working on my desires.

Honestly, none of the results from that profile were surprising; I knew what I excelled at and what gave me satisfaction. But I had never stopped long enough to consider incorporating those strengths more directly and intentionally in my life or work. For fifty years, I had taken the path of least resistance, doing what my friends were doing, taking the advice of my parents, making decisions based on what I thought was expected of me, and following the crowd. Those decisions were based on the *what* but never on the *who*.

The DISC Profile armed me with information and a way to articulate what made me tick—what made me who I was and what made me unique. I took that information and committed to using it to live into my strengths, which meant I had to look into my future and decide what was next for my life. Around the same time, my dad retired from his career at Texas A&M and proposed that we start a consulting business together. *Okay, wait. Time out!* I thought. *Here I am trying to create my own path and avoid doing what my dad suggests.* This time, though, I understood more about myself and what I wanted out of life. And truth be told, I really liked the idea of starting a business and working with my dad. As we mapped out what our company could look like, I could see how consulting would allow me to use my strengths. It would require me to develop relationships with clients, whom I could then coach so they could help their organizations succeed. Talk about a custom fit!

It has been several years since I took that assessment, and the clarity it gave me has made a huge difference in my life. I feel more confident in my choices—choices that I make deliberately based on what I am designed to do and who I am called to be. I experience far fewer moments of indecision and second-guessing because I am intentionally enjoying the life that God uniquely designed for me.

What Makes You Who You Are?

So, what about you? How well do you know yourself?

One of life's biggest challenges is understanding who you are—your likes, dislikes, strengths, weaknesses, preferences, and opinions. Peer and cultural pressure can be extreme. Maybe you have gotten used to going with the flow, following the crowd, or making choices based on others' expectations. Maybe you have been so busy, distracted, or complacent that you've never stopped to consider what unique personality traits, characteristics, and qualities make you who you are.

I'll promise you this: You have been uniquely designed. You are a limited edition. You have God-given traits and abilities that set you apart from others and set you up for a life of purpose and meaning. Do you know what those traits and abilities are?

If not, I encourage you to take the time to consider your strengths, weaknesses, desires, and opinions. It is a worthwhile investment of your time to take a personality assessment. The cost is minimal (and in some cases free), and the information you gain could prove to be an excellent guide to move you in a God-given direction. Discovering what you want—what your driving desires are—will prove helpful throughout the remainder of your life. But first things first. To know your desires, you must first understand *who* you are.

Do not go where the path may lead; go instead where there is no path and leave a trail.
—Ralph Waldo Emerson

More Questions to Consider

❏ Do you feel like you know yourself and what you want out of life?

❏ What are your strengths, weaknesses, likes, and dislikes?

❏ If those are difficult to answer, would you be willing to take a personal inventory or personality assessment to better understand yourself?

Here are a few options:

- Meyers-Briggs Assessment (free)—16Personalities.com
- DISC Personality Profile (fee)—DiscProfile.com
- CliftonStrengths (fee)—store.gallup.com
- Enneagram (free)—YourEnneagramCoach.com

ARE YOU PAYING ATTENTION?

To be above average demands a choice. It requires that we defy the odds. You have no control of whether you have been endowed with above average talent or intelligence or physical attributes. What you can control is whether you choose to live your life defined and determined by the status quo.

—Erwin McManus, *The Last Arrow*

How did you get this far in life?

What paths did you take or choices did you make that landed you at this place at this time, reading this book?

Can you retrace your steps? Were they deliberate, or have you been just putting one foot in front of the other?

You have probably heard the phrase, "If you don't know where you're going, any road will get you there." Maybe there's some truth to that quip, but I also believe that if you are living with your eternal purpose in mind, God may well be directing your steps without you being aware of it.

Thank goodness for that!

I've already admitted to you that making decisions wasn't my strongest trait in my younger days. Looking back on many of the decisions that ultimately determined my path, it seems like my choices were not just unplanned or unstructured; they were downright haphazard.

Let me share a little more of my story so you can see what I mean: My friends and I grew up in a traditional, American, Christian home. Our happily married parents took us to church every Sunday morning, Sunday night, and Wednesday night. We played outside after school and ate family supper at the table most nights. Summers came with lots of free time (unless you played Little League baseball) and maybe a family vacation. In short, my childhood was simple, stress-free, easy, and practically void of the need to make any real decisions. And any decision I did have to make, I made nonchalantly. I didn't worry about making the right decision or the best decision; I simply decided and moved on, reasonably sure that everything would work out. Because everything always had.

Before I go on, I want to pause and acknowledge that I'm aware that the picture this paints is one of a well-sheltered, upper-middle-class, suburban childhood. I don't apologize for that. But I also understand that not everyone (especially today's children) experienced such a simple childhood. Regardless, our experiences, families, neighbors, friends, and circumstances all factor into the people we become as adults.

It wasn't until my senior year of high school that I had to start making any real decisions, and even those were heavily influenced by my friends or family. I only needed four classes that year to graduate. A friend of mine was working half days; it seemed like a good idea, so I attended morning classes and worked afternoons.

As that final school year wound down, my dad suggested I take a job for a self-employed business owner who was looking for summer help drilling water wells. The job included room and board because work was often daylight to dark and was an hour's drive away. Among my friends, summer jobs were common. Working out of town, however, was an exception. Since my father suggested it, and it seemed like an adventure, I was for it. Why not? Decision made! Easy! I graduated on a Friday night and started work the following Monday.

The following fall, I started attending classes at Texas A&M University. I mentioned in the previous chapter that my buddy Mike and I chose to go to A&M in large part because our fathers had done so. When they were students, it was an all-male, all-military school. Around the time A&M admitted females (1964–65), the military requirement also became non-compulsory. The military tradition continued as an organization known as the Corps of Cadets. Since our fathers had been in the Corps, Mike and I dared each other to join. It was a test of toughness.

I made a four-year commitment based on my father's example and the influence of a friend, not once stopping to consider whether joining the Corps was something I actually wanted. I have no regrets whatsoever about the choice; my experience in the Corps introduced me to lifelong friends and helped me develop discipline and self-confidence. But once again, it was a decision to which I gave little thought.

Toward the end of my sophomore year, I had to decide whether to take a military contract, which varied in length but typically was at least a four-year commitment, or go D&C (Drills & Ceremonies), which signified those students who were in the Corps their junior and senior years but not under a military contract. This was one of the first times I had trouble making a decision. Honestly, I knew I was not the military type, but the Army paid $100 a month during the junior and senior years, so I went with the contract.

Yes, really.

Money was the swaying factor in the decision I regretted almost immediately.

One of the requirements for the Army contract was to attend a six-week, summer, military training camp in Fort Riley, Kansas. Evidently, there was a surplus of students during the summer of 1982 because I failed to pass the physical exam due to a torn tendon in a finger on my left hand and was sent home. I felt a true sense of relief receiving an Honorable Discharge.

On the long drive home from Kansas to Texas, I had plenty of time to think, but I have no memory of being concerned for how I would spend the remainder of the summer. And it turned out there was no need to worry. The director of Camp Deer Run, a Christian camp located in Northeast Texas, had left a message for me to call him. I did and found out he wanted to know if I could fill in—starting immediately—for a counselor who was out with an injury. Since I had no plans and working at a summer camp sounded like fun, of course, I was interested! No real decision to make. My summer was now planned.

Working at camp was a great fit. The director asked me to stay the entire summer. I agreed and absolutely enjoyed it. I came back the following summer as the camp's program director and wished I could stay on in a full-time capacity. But when that summer ended, I found myself as a college graduate with three months of work experience and no further plans.

You'd think it would be time for a serious decision, right?

Well, sort of.

When I arrived home at the end of the summer, my dad asked about my plans and whether I had any interest in working at Abilene Christian University (ACU). A man he worked for at Pepperdine University was now President at ACU. My father had learned a lot and had a great experience working for this man, so he figured it would also be good training for me. Dad called and inquired about opportunities, I went in for an interview, and shortly thereafter, I started at ACU as Assistant to the President.

Dad was right. I did learn a lot; I learned about Alumni Relations and Development. Later, I served as a director for Camp Kadesh and eventually moved into a position in ACU's University Advancement Office. ACU is also where I met Amy, the girl who would later become my wife.

Here I was, a young professional on a college campus, involved at a local church, dating a great Christian girl, yet still feeling unsettled about my life. I liked working at ACU, but I did not enjoy my work. Also, because I felt like my job was my dad's suggestion rather than the result of any personal desire or calling, I didn't feel a sense of ownership or commitment. The problem was, I did not know what I wanted to do.

What to Do When You Don't Know What to Do

After a year and a half at ACU, I knew I needed to make a change, so I took a mission internship in Bangkok, Thailand. I would be working under Kelly Davidson and Larry Henderson, men I had come to admire. I had known Kelly for years, and our families were close. Larry and I had become acquaintances through mutual friends. After a year together in Thailand, we developed a close friendship that continues to this day. That internship gave me some space from the day-to-day drift I had fallen into. The mission made me see myself and the world in a new way, and I enjoyed learning a new language, teaching English, working with Thai children, and even coaching Little League. From this time in Thailand, I learned that **when you don't know what to do, you can't go wrong choosing to work with good people doing something you know is worthwhile.**

I'd been in Thailand for almost a year when my life—my whole family's life—took a sharp turn. I received word that one of my younger brothers, Richard, had been in a serious car accident on the way home from a school-related camping trip at Enchanted Rock State Park. He and five other guys from his Outdoor Recreation Class had ridden together, and on the return trip, only a few miles from home, the driver made a U-turn. Their car was broadsided by an eighteen-wheeler, and three of the students died instantly. One passed later that night, and my brother, at twenty-two years old, and one other young man survived.

Richard hung on for three excruciating months in a comatose existence—the hardest three months of my and my family's lives. When he passed, I experienced a moment of clarity. I suppose Richard's death made me realize that life was too short and precious to just drift. Whatever the reason, I finally knew what I *wanted* to do: teach math and coach.

That may sound like a decision pulled out of the clear blue sky, but let's retrace my steps to see why it made sense. After working at Camp Deer Run for two summers, at Camp Kadesh at ACU, and then working with children and students in Thailand, I knew I wanted to be involved with kids. I had also developed an appreciation for math. My maternal grandfather had taught math at both the high school and college level his entire career. (He even tutored me on a few occasions as I began working part-time and taking classes in order to obtain a teaching certificate in math.) Putting the two things together just made sense to me.

Making such a huge shift in my career was not easy, but I was up to the challenge because it was what I wanted to do. I went back to school and earned a teacher certification. On the recommendation of my future brother-in-law, Brad McCoy, who was head football coach and athletic director in San Saba, Texas, at the time, I attended the Texas High

School Coaches Association's annual Coaching School to find job connections. At Coaching School, school districts post openings on a job board. Brady Independent School District needed a math teacher and junior high coach, and I needed a place to start. We were a match, and I headed to Brady, the Heart of Texas and home of the Bulldogs! For the first time, I felt a real passion and excitement for my work.

In hindsight, I now see God's hand guiding me through each and every decision. Where I would work, the people I would meet along the way, and even discovering my desires were all at His direction. Was I aware of His Spirit leading me? Not at the time, but I can look back and see that He was by my side and involved in each decision.

Is God Working in Your Life?

"Be still, and know that I am God." You may be familiar with those words from Psalm 46. Just before them, the writer comments on God's power and steady control through times of natural disaster and war.

It is a challenge for me to "be still" in moments of change or chaos. Can you relate? But the message of Psalm 46 is clear: Be still. Pay attention. Look around and notice God's power and His provision.

To really understand what God is doing or has done, you have to be still. Often it is easier for me to see God's leading upon reflection, months and even years after the fact. Looking back, I can see how God clearly led me to the right people, places, and decisions. But is it possible to see

... I PRESS ON ...

I DO NOT CONSIDER MYSELF
YET TO HAVE TAKEN HOLD
OF IT. BUT ONE THING I DO:
FORGETTING WHAT IS BEHIND
AND STRAINING TOWARD WHAT
IS AHEAD, I PRESS ON TOWARD
THE GOAL ...

—THE APOSTLE PAUL, PHILIPPIANS 3:12–14 (NIV)

Him working in your life in the present? Perhaps, but as the psalmist suggests, being still is a requirement.

Although I only taught math and coached four years, I would not trade it. I was able to be an example to many students and players. I helped them learn and provided encouragement, inspiration, and at times, pushed them toward their potential. Since my years as a teacher, I have enjoyed several different roles, but I'm curious if I might have been able to teach and coach longer had I been paying attention, listening to my heart, and looking at my strengths.

More Questions to Consider

❑ Reflect on the path you have taken in life. Are you satisfied or are you regretful?

❑ What are the things keeping you from making better decisions and being more intentional about where you're going?

❑ How can you include God's direction in your decisions?

HOW DO YOU CHOOSE?

You have brains in your head.
You have feet in your shoes.
You can steer yourself any direction you choose.

—Dr. Seuss, *Oh, The Places You'll Go*

Life is a series of choices. Some are inconsequential and others determine the direction of your life.

I have already admitted to you that I've made plenty of decisions—sometimes major decisions—without much thought or deliberation. That was especially true for me as a teen and young adult. I often did what my friends were doing or followed my father's advice. I have few regrets, not because every choice was spot on, but because I've been able to learn something even when they weren't the best choices. I can look back and see how God has blessed the choices I've made, using even the wrong turns to keep me on His path.

Things have turned out fine for me, but I do wonder how my life might have been different had I taken time to consider my options and what I really desired out of life. What might I have done differently had I paused earlier in my life to investigate strengths and talents and how they could be integral in my daily work? I'm not going to lose sleep over it, but I do wonder.

I spent much of my life on the "ready-fire-aim" end of the decision-making spectrum. On the other end of that spectrum are the people who over-analyze and overthink their options until the decision becomes obsolete. I worked with a principal in a Christian school who illustrates this point. Any time his teachers would come to him asking for help with a decision, his standard answer was, "Let me pray about it and get back to you." Now, the teachers weren't asking him to decide. They simply wanted his counsel so they could make the best decision. Maybe he really was praying about how to answer, but his pattern of behavior seemed more like a stall tactic that got him out of having to make or even contribute to decisions. More often than not, by the time he finally offered an opinion, the teachers had already made the decision and moved on.

So we have the too-quick decision makers, the non-deciders, and then there are the people who cannot seem to make a good decision to save their lives. I know more than a couple of guys who seem cursed with the inability to make a good decision. From the girls they dated in college, to friends they chose to surround them as peers, to their decisions on marriage, children, and work, it seems as though they have consistently made bad decisions. You probably know someone who fits that category, too, and maybe you wonder if that person will ever learn how to make good decisions.

Which brings up the question: Can *anyone* learn to make good decisions?

Here's the good news: The answer is *Yes!*

The bad news is that the learning process takes time. With practice, trial and error, and a willingness to grow from the wrong decisions, I believe anyone can learn to make good decisions. Or perhaps more accurately stated, anyone who wants to learn to make good decisions has the ability to do so.

So are you ready to learn?

How Can I Learn to Choose Wisely?

There are all sorts of ways to make decisions, from the thoughtless (flipping a coin) to the time-consuming (taking a poll). Rather than leaving things to chance or asking for everyone's opinion, one suggestion and my preference these days is a simple process like this one outlined by Kescia D. Gray of GrayKo Clinical Consultants and published in *Corporate Wellness Magazine*:

- **Identify Your Goal**
- **Gather Information for Weighing Options**
- **Consider the Consequences**
- **Make Your Decision**
- **Evaluate Your Decision**

Identify Your Goal

This step seems obvious, but it's amazing how many people don't stop to consider what they really want to do. Timing may be forcing you into a decision, or you may simply be ready for a change.

> **Example:** *You're nearing high school graduation, and people are asking about your plans. Do you have any?*

Gather Information for Weighing Options

Take a look at all your options and start eliminating the things you know aren't right for you. Think of it like a multiple-choice question on an exam. When you don't know the correct answer, what do you do? You eliminate the responses that you know to be incorrect, thereby reducing the odds of choosing the wrong answer and increasing the odds of selecting the correct answer.

> **Example:** *Let's say you were about to graduate from high school, and your choices included a military commitment, continued study (community college, trade school, or university), work, or a combination of working and studying. There would likely be at least one of those you could eliminate. If you know you are not ready for college because you have no idea what to study and, therefore, the investment of time and money seems like a waste, then you have narrowed the field to military or working.*

Consider the Consequences

This step could be as simple as listing the pros and cons, or you might want to create a more elaborate table including expectations or predictions for one year, two years, and five years out.

> **Example:** *If you've narrowed down your post-high school options to trade school, community college, or university, then list the pros and cons of each decision. A few factors that you might list to help make the best decision include costs, admission requirements, duration to complete a degree, and even social life.*

Make Your Decision

Once you have gathered the data and considered the consequences, the best choice should be obvious or at least more apparent.

> **Example:** *If the cost of education is a major factor and you like the idea of learning a skill and getting to work, then trade school could be the easy decision. Your reasoning might be simple: You can start earning a paycheck sooner rather than later while you continue to evaluate your interest in a community college or university degree.*

Evaluate Your Decision

Once you make a major decision, don't act on it immediately. Sleep on it overnight and then share your plans with a few trusted friends or mentors who know you well.

Example: *Tell your friends or mentors that you are considering trade school. Share your reasons and how you came to the decision and then ask for their feedback. They might be able to provide additional insight to either affirm your decision or cause you to reconsider.*

Is the Timing Right?

Regardless of which process or decision-making model you use, timing is a consideration. Ask: *Is this a decision I need to be making now?* If the answer is no, when would be the appropriate time? For example, you may be absolutely driven to plan your next vacation; however, the trip is a year away. So much can change in a year! Planning the details for your trip too early could actually end up being a waste of time and money. The best choice might be to select a date at which it would make more sense to begin deciding and planning.

Finally and most importantly, pray over the pending decision. Even if it is a quick or rushed decision, ask God to provide wisdom and discernment.

Commit to the Lord whatever you do, and he will establish your plans.
—Solomon, Proverbs 16:3 (NIV)

Plans fail for lack of counsel, but with many advisers they succeed.
—Solomon, Proverbs 15:22 (NIV)

MANY ARE THE PLANS IN A PERSON'S HEART, BUT IT IS THE LORD'S PURPOSE THAT PREVAILS.

—SOLOMON, PROVERBS 19:21 (NIV)

In his book, *Blink: The Power of Thinking without Thinking*, Malcolm Gladwell delineates between conscious and unconscious decision-making. He provides several examples of the power of our adaptive unconscious thinking, a seemingly instant mental process for deciphering information without engaging the conscious mind. Gladwell writes, "We are innately suspicious of this kind of rapid cognition. We live in a world that assumes that the quality of a decision is directly related to the time and effort that went into making it." Experience and research, however, give some weight to the concept of unconscious decision-making. Gladwell explains in *Blink* that time is not the most essential factor for good decisions. He suggests:

- **Decisions made quickly can be as good as those made cautiously and deliberately.** For example, let's consider making the most of your eight-hour workday and getting the most important things done. If you give it no thought, there is a good chance calls, texts, emails, and checking social media on your phone will prove to be distractions. Next thing you know the day is over, you have not finished what you intended, and it may mean staying late to finish your work.

- **Sometimes you need to trust your instincts.** If you waste time at work, you'll have to stay late to finish up. That reality alone should cause you to prioritize your time and efforts, but some realities are easy to ignore. Staying late may not cause you much concern, but what about the threat of losing your job? Missed deadlines and poor time management just might cost you the job! When your unconscious brain registers the possibility of no work, which leads to no money and no place to live, it sounds an alarm that forces you to focus on what's important, rather than on urgent but less important distractions like social media.

- **Snap judgments and first impressions can be educated and controlled.** With enough practice and repetition, you may subconsciously make a priority list to start each week, perhaps each workday. The question you will automatically find yourself addressing is, "What do I have to get done today?"

Not long ago, Alex Carstens, a medical student and the son of a good friend, spoke at our church about some of the things he has learned about the brain and our conscious and subconscious decision-making abilities. Interested in what he said, I followed up and asked him to share more about what he is learning. This strikes me as crucial information, and I think we should all be paying attention, even if we aren't in med school.

Alex shared that the only things you really control in your body are your voluntary skeletal movements and your conscious thoughts. The rest of your body's systems and processes, including your subconscious thoughts, are *not* under your direct control. You can't make your heart beat, stomach digest, immune system resist infection, or control the chemical reactions related to emotions by thinking about them. All of those things listed, though not under our direct control, *are* within our *indirect* control.

For example, you cannot simply concentrate on your heart and directly increase or decrease its rate. But you can increase your heart rate by focusing on things you fear or worry about. In the same way, you can slow your heart rate by calming your mind and taking a few slow, deep breaths, which means, you can *indirectly* affect your heart rate.

Similarly, you cannot just think and *directly* control your white blood cells (as if we'd even know how), but you can *indirectly* affect your immune system. Stress and smoking—both things you are able to control—can negatively affect your immune system. Eating a healthy diet and getting enough sleep are indirect ways that you can positively influence your immune system.

Your subconscious mind works similarly to those processes. It is not directly in your control, but you can control it indirectly. You can do that by using your conscious thoughts and actions to train your unconscious mind. And it is vital that you be intentional about training your subconscious mind. Because as Alex commented, "Satan wants us to struggle helplessly against deeply rooted habits and things out of our control rather than focus intently on what we *can* control."

Habits. Tendencies. Addictions. We all have them. They are the behaviors and thoughts that we don't have to think about. We just do them, over and over again.

There are good habits and there are habits that can wreck our lives.

One common subconscious habit (affliction) is phone addiction. In case you're thinking that I'm about to launch into a tirade about the younger generation who seem tied to their phones, I need to say this first: Hi, I'm Sid, and I'm a phone addict. If you are like me and cannot say, "Today I won't reflexively or obsessively check my phone and scroll through social media" because you know you are very likely to pick up your phone without realizing it, you might be a phone addict too. Our subconscious habit has us checking our phones at least every ten minutes, according to a recent survey by Asurion—that's up to ninety-six times a day!

Breaking any bad habit or addiction is difficult, and this one is no exception. But it is possible. The tactics you use to re-train your subconscious brain regarding your phone can also be applied to changing other subconscious behavior.

Set up Speedbumps or Roadblocks

Speedbumps shake you out of autopilot mode. Changing your passcode, for instance, will make you stop and think when you pick up your phone. That pause is often just long enough to help you make a conscious decision to put it back down. Speedbumps like the following can be useful for breaking other negative habits:

- Set blockers on your phone and computer for porn websites.
- Avoid buying junk food so it is not easily accessible when you get a craving.
- Disable the internet on your phone for twenty-four hours.

- Enlist accountability partners to provide regular check-ins.

Change Your Environment

If your phone is the last thing you see before sleeping and the first thing you see when waking up, you are training your subconscious to value and depend on your phone instead of reinforcing the habits you genuinely want. I think this is a reason the Bible tells us to fill our hearts with the Word and prayer first thing in the morning and last thing at night—bookending our day to reinforce chosen values to the subconscious mind.

- Sleep with your phone in another room.
- Place your Bible next to the coffee pot.
- Keep a journal on your nightstand.

Reinforce Positive Choices

Removing temptations works to prevent or eliminate negative behaviors, but it is important to find ways to promote and affirm good choices. Positive reinforcements go a long way to promote behaviors you would like to reinforce, reward, and renew.

- When you open your Bible, remind yourself of three benefits before you start reading.
- Spend time encouraging others in areas where you need help (self-reinforcing).
- At the end of each day, write down three positive accomplishments.

**In the morning, Lord, you hear my voice;
in the morning I lay my requests before you.**
—David, Psalms 5:3 (NIV)

**. . . proclaiming your love in the morning
and your faithfulness at night.**
—David, Psalms 92:2 (NIV)

**I will praise the Lord, who counsels me;
even at night my heart instructs me.**
—David, Psalms 16:7 (NIV)

The Apostle Paul offers this bizarre but fundamental statement in the book of Romans, lamenting the paradox of our decisions being outside of our direct control:

> *For I have the desire to do what is good, but I cannot carry it out. For I do not do the good I want to do, but the evil I do not want to do—this I keep on doing*
>
> —Romans 7:18–19 (NIV)

How could this be true unless there is something making our decisions for us? In the next verse, he identifies this force as "sin living in me" (Romans 7:20, NIV). I would say that one mechanism by which sin can "live in us" is by hijacking our subconscious habits and inclining us towards selfishness, laziness, or pride. But the Bible is also clear that this can be overcome. Paul says in 1 Corinthians 9:27, "I beat my body and make it my slave," which implies both that our bodies *can* be outside of our control and that we *can* regain control. I think one purpose of the emphasis in the early church on regular fasting, giving, teaching, meeting, and praying is to reinforce our chosen values to our subconscious mind. To avoid being ruled by habits and circumstances, Christians make repeated intentional decisions that shape our hearts, as well as decisions toward heaven.

Major decisions can define you and determine your future. Choices about what you believe regarding spiritual matters, whether to attend college, which college, whether to get married, whom you marry, choices on work, and decisions regarding family and friends all have an impact on the path you take and outcomes you will experience. Daily decisions, such as what to eat, how much to exercise, or how well you use your time also factor into the kind of life and health you enjoy.

Want a better life—a better quality of life? Start making better decisions. It truly is that simple. Perhaps not easy, but simple.

More Questions to Consider

❑ How well have you done making decisions?

❑ Are you satisfied with your decision track record?

❑ What major decisions are coming in the near future?

❑ Are you willing to take your time and use a decision process?

❑ Which trusted friends can you enlist for advice?

❑ Will you regularly ask God through prayer to help you make better decisions?

WHAT WILL YOU MAKE OF YOUR MISTAKES?

If any of you lacks wisdom, you should ask God, who gives generously to all without finding fault, and it will be given to you.

—James 1:5 (NIV)

When we're young, it's easy to fall into the trap of thinking we have life all figured out. If you've already survived one or more of the life stages below, you are acquainted with the risks of brash (and baseless) confidence.

- At age sixteen, armed with a driver's license, you're an expert behind the wheel—until you get your first speeding ticket or worse, experience your first auto accident.
- At age twenty-one, able to legally drink alcohol, you're a confident adult—until you drink too

much and say or do something you regret for years to come.

- Fresh out of college, you know it all—until you get your first full-time job and make a poor decision at work that has lasting negative consequences.
- As a young adult, you get married to the love of your life and think you have the perfect lifelong relationship—until your first real argument when words are used as weapons and end up cutting deep.
- As a young parent, you are convinced you're raising the model child—until the first public tantrum makes it clear that you can't control the situation or avoid embarrassment.

Wisdom comes from more than a rite of passage, the collection of information, or simply crossing the next threshold along the timeline in your life. Wisdom is the result of hard work; it comes from experience, and it takes time. Lots of time.

Exactly how much time depends on you—on what you put into learning and what you do with mistakes you make along the way.

In *Outliers*, Malcolm Gladwell writes about the 10,000-Hour Rule, citing research that indicates "ten thousand hours of practice is required to achieve the level of mastery associated with being a world-class expert—in anything."

Exactly how long is that? If you put in eight hours a day, five days a week, you would achieve mastery in about five years. But when we're talking about mastery of a skill, like managing your money, or even a hobby, like golf, a more likely scenario would be that mastery might take upwards of ten years. You're not practicing those skills eight hours a day. If we're talking about developing the wisdom to navigate relationships, like marriage or parenting, mastery could take a lifetime.

That is a lot of time invested and likely many mistakes made in the learning process.

The Upside of Mistakes

Mistakes. No one wants to make them, and yet *experience* comes as a result of learning from mistakes. The problem is that we often have such a strong fear of failure that we stick to the safe route to minimize mistakes and avoid failure. And *that's* a mistake.

I have often admired the trait of being able to make a quick decision. When I was in college, I recall receiving more than one invitation to a meal, plus I wanted to exercise, although I knew that what I really needed to do was study. It was a tough spot for me, and I was absolutely perplexed because I did not want to choose; I wanted to do them all! With some maturity, I was soon able to make those types of simple choices quickly.

Big decisions, however, can present an entirely different dilemma. One bad decision regarding who to date, taking the wrong job, or making an investment and losing money can cause you to develop a serious fear of failure. The reaction is often to play it safe and avoid making big decisions at all for fear of making the wrong choice.

In his book, *Attitude: Develop a Winning Mindset On and Off The Court*, Jay Wright, Villanova Head Basketball Coach, offers this advice:

> *Never fear failure. Think of it as an opportunity to learn. If you can approach every challenge without a fear of failure, knowing that you'll learn from any setback, you will find it easier to work with a free and uncluttered mind.*

Mistakes are fine, as long as we learn from them and find a way to prevent their repetition. Case in point: A lesson I learned from a mistake I made early in my professional life sticks with me even today. I had been asked to share a few thoughts at a special chapel session on the Friday night before ACU's homecoming game. I had been a regular speaker at camp the previous summer and had enjoyed teaching Sunday school classes, so I was confident I could handle the speaking opportunity without much preparation—until I was introduced that evening in Moody Coliseum.

As I stepped onto the gym floor and looked up into the stands full of college students, panic punched me in the gut. My throat suddenly felt dry, my hands shook, and my mind went blank. I took a deep breath, opened my mouth, and thankfully, words did in fact come out. I don't remember what I said, and neither, I'm sure, does anyone else because the message I delivered that night came across as completely underwhelming.

I knew immediately that I should have prepared. Lesson learned. The hard way.

As a result of that mistake, I get that bad-gut feeling every time I'm asked to speak. The quick jolt of panic serves as a reminder of the need for, and importance of, preparation. I learned my lesson, and the wisdom I gained continues to motivate me. I now set aside ample time to prepare for any speaking engagement so that I can walk away confident that I did my best.

When we choose to learn from mistakes, our behaviors change, which is a sure sign of wisdom and growing from experience. Looking back at the examples shared at the opening of the chapter, consider how experience can prompt us to develop positive habits to avoid repeating mistakes:

- You might develop a mental checklist to review prior to driving, in order to drive more safely and perhaps more slowly to avoid a future ticket or accident.
- You set limits for yourself when drinking, if at all, and decide beforehand what action to take when you are encouraged and tempted to drink more.
- You take ownership of your work and create a to-do list in order to ensure you perform well on the job.
- You commit to thinking *before* speaking to your spouse, especially in times of conflict. And when miscommunications occur, you immediately apologize and work toward a solution.
- You might help your children practice expected proper behavior at home to avoid future meltdowns.

Mistakes can be beneficial, and they are often how we learn. By forming good habits and developing healthy routines as a result of our mistakes, we can train ourselves to avoid unhealthy choices and drive our behavior toward improvement and growth.

We all deal with setbacks but in the long run, the quality of our lives often depends on the quality of our habits. With the same habits, you'll end up with the same results. But with better habits, anything is possible.

—James Clear, Atomic Habits

More Questions to Consider

❑ What is one mistake in your life that was a life lesson to learn from?

❑ Has it caused you to develop healthy habits or positive routines?

❑ What other past mistake can you turn into an opportunity to improve?

6

WHAT AND WHO INFLUENCE YOU?

You will be the same person in five years as you are today except for the people you meet and the books you read.
—Charlie Jones, *Life Is Tremendous!*

One summer near the end of college, I ended up stranded on a friend's farm in Kansas. The car I had driven there needed a new gas tank, and the repairs were going to take almost a week. I mowed the grass and did a few other jobs to help earn my keep, but when the chores were done, I had nothing to do. My friend introduced me to author Louis L'Amour through a paperback.

Up to that point in my life, I hadn't been a reader. I distinctly remember feeling embarrassed as a child because I was a slow reader, and I avoided reading out loud in school at all costs. If assignments in high school required reading, I rarely completed them. I even quit buying textbooks in college when I realized it was a waste of money; I *never* read them.

But that day, out of a combination of boredom and politeness, I took the book and started following the words and turning the pages. Lying in bed that night, I could not put down the book. I was captivated! Finally, at 2:00 a.m., I decided I had better get some sleep.

For the first time in my life, I realized I enjoyed reading. What had made the difference? Perhaps the fact that the book wasn't *required*. More likely, it was the discovery of a book's ability to transport me into another world. I was not simply reading words on a page; I felt like I was in the story.

Today it almost seems that books are old-fashioned. (I'm very happy you picked up this one, by the way.) We live in a rapid-paced world of information condensed into headlines and 280 characters or less. Everything you need to know can be obtained online in a matter of seconds. A fact which begs the question, is it *really* that important to read books?

For me, the answer is yes for a few different reasons. First, there's the connection between reading, education, and income. A 2019 study by Andrew Perrin of Pew Research found that 27 percent of adults in the U.S. had not read a book (print, online, or audio) in the past year.

The same study revealed that these non-book readers were much more likely to be less-educated (high school diploma or less) and lower-income individuals (annual household income $30,000 or less) than their book-reading counterparts. One thing may or may not cause the other, but if you want to educate yourself and increase your earning potential, you can't go wrong by reading books!

It's true that we can access information in a variety of non-book formats, but the benefits of reading books go beyond acquiring information. In her article, "The Life-Long Benefits of Reading for Pleasure," Alice Sullivan shares that children who read for fun on a regular basis showed significant intellectual progress (four times greater!) in vocabulary, spelling, and math. In a follow-up study with the same group of almost 10,000 people, reading continued to be a valuable part of their lives as adults, and they showed large gains in vocabulary between ages sixteen and forty-two.

Alan Castel, PhD, shares that reading throughout your lifetime promotes social intelligence, preserves mental ability, decreases physical signs of dementia, improves social benefits, and increases memory. In addition, children who grew up in homes with books, regardless of their parents' education and income levels, achieved higher levels of education.

The magic of reading is that it allows you to escape current challenges and struggles to enter another world through story. Fiction or non-fiction, biography or business, history or future, the power of story captures the imagination so that the picture you see is yours and completely unique. This is why books are better for your brain than movies: You see what your mind creates, not what a filmmaker wants you to see. Your imagination is a powerful tool.

I finished that first Louis L'Amour book, and then I picked up another that he had written, and then another. Later I started reading John Grisham's novels one by one. When I find novelists whose writing styles I enjoy, I stick with them! The same is true for non-fiction. I enjoy reading books by Mark Batterson, Malcolm Gladwell, Jon Gordon, John Krakauer, Eric Metaxas, Donald Miller, and Simon Sinek. Gordon, Metaxas, and Miller write from a Christian perspective that provides inspiration for my professional and personal success. Batterson is a Christian author whose books encourage me to live with a stronger faith.

Jon Gordon's story continues to inspire me with hope and purpose. He was struggling at work, which I believe was in sales. In fact, he hated his job, and it was affecting his entire life. In his book, *The Power of Positive Leadership*, he writes, "By the age of 31, I was a fearful, negative, stressed-out, and miserable husband and father to two young children. My wife had had enough. She gave me an ultimatum: Change or our marriage was over."

From that moment, he began reading everything he could find on positive psychology. He was drawn to encouraging and motivating others, which led him to write his first book, *The Energy Bus*. But in his heart, his passion was to become a motivational speaker. He shares that only four people signed up for his first training, but he stayed positive and gave them his very best. He knew they all had friends, and if he could inspire those four, then word would spread, groups would grow, his work would increase, and he could become a legitimate motivational speaker.

In addition to being a well-known speaker, he has written twenty-three books. His story inspires me because he did not give up and decided to change, grow, and improve. It started with changing his attitude to become a positive person in all he did. Jon is a living example that we can set a goal, work toward it, and achieve it.

Bottom line: Reading transforms you. It makes you consider different perspectives. Long-form reading, like books, engages and challenges your brain in a way that the blogs, social media, and memes cannot. But a word of warning: Be careful what you read! Just like anything in the world today, there's good and bad, so be wise and discerning in your choices. Reading can indeed transform you, but it holds the power to make you positive or negative. Be intentional about what you read and make sure it is to your advantage personally, professionally, and most important, eternally.

Even if you don't consider yourself a reader, I challenge you to find a book that captivates or inspires you. If you have a long, daily commute, listen to an audio book. Whatever you do, read! If you read one book a year, you're reading more than the average American. But don't settle on being average.

If one book has the power to transform you, imagine the possibilities if you committed to reading one book a month or more?

Make it happen.

I guess there are never enough books.
—John Steinbeck

I kept two books in my pocket,
one to read, one to write in.
—Robert Louis Stevenson

You can never get a cup of tea large enough
or a book long enough to suit me.
—C.S. Lewis

Today a reader, tomorrow a leader.
—Margaret Fuller

Books are a uniquely portable magic.
—Stephen King

Who's in Your Contact List?

If books have the ability to change you, how much more of an impact do "the people you meet" have on your life?

Before we dive into answering that question, let's define "the people you meet" as those who fall into the following categories:

- **Introductions** are people you have met but may not recall their names.
- **Acquaintances** are people you see on a regular basis and know their name.

- **Friends** are people with whom you spend time, both in good and bad circumstances.
- **Mentors** are often people older and wiser than you who are able to share from their experiences.

The people who have the greatest impact on our lives are our friends and mentors. These are the people who fulfill Charlie Jones's prediction by causing us to grow and improve.

Closer than a Brother

Friends can be close for a season or for a lifetime. These are the people, typically peers, with whom you have laughed, cried, and made memories.

But in this age of social media and online "friends," you may doubt whether you really need friends in the flesh. Could it be that the need for real-life friends is fading and becoming a thing of the past?

Not if you're wise.

Even though we are more connected than ever, unhappiness is at an all-time high, and as a result, the suicide rate is escalating. The challenges created by the COVID-19 virus in 2020, including social distancing, the closing of schools, churches, and business, and mandated telecommuting, have left us feeling more disconnected than ever. Is it any wonder that isolation has become an even bigger crisis? Living our lives even more online-dependent, where comparison produces depression, we need true friends in the flesh more than ever.

Whether it's a shoulder to cry on, a hand to hold, or simply someone to listen, everyone needs a friend they can count on. Like the old Bill Withers song says, "we *all* need somebody to lean on."

So, who's your friend? Whom do you call when tragedy strikes?

Does someone immediately come to mind? Maybe a best friend, perhaps someone you know has your back, no matter how dire the circumstances.

If so, great! Take care of that relationship. Make time to check in and touch base. Even better, spend time together in real life doing something you both enjoy. For me, that could be as simple as catching up over a cup of coffee. But doesn't it seem like food brings out the best in us? Sharing a meal, especially in a home, can be the secret ingredient in rich friendships. The menu is unimportant. The key is breaking bread together in the comfort of a home. There are fewer interruptions, and the atmosphere is relaxed, most of the time.

If no one immediately comes to mind as your go-to friend but you want to develop that kind of close-knit friendship, you know what to do, right? *Be* a friend. Some of the best advice I have heard and try to practice when it comes to building friendships is, "If you want a friend, you've got to be a friend!"

It's not always fun, it's not always fair, and it can get messy. But that's real life, and it's true of any relationship in which you risk investing yourself. Developing and nurturing strong relationships is worth the effort. When crisis hits, you need people you can rely on. We were made for community. No matter how independent we think we are, we need other people.

Between semesters of my sophomore year, one of my classmates and Corps unit members, John Nisbet, Jr. (aka Nez), lost his roommate. I moved in with him and quickly discovered Nez to be gregarious, hilarious, and a strong believer in God. Prior to living with Nez, I occasionally showed my personality, but only with those I knew well. Nez's example of living out loud with full confidence, courage, and boldness for God, regardless of the company or location, inspired me. I credit much of the positive personality and can-do attitude I live with today to Nez.

Soon after graduation, Nez began his commitment as a Marine. After stops at Quantico, Pensacola, and San Diego, he was stationed at the Marine base in Hawaii. It was there that his helicopter went down on a test flight. I will be forever grateful to Nez for the memories and laughter we shared and for his example that continues to inspire me. I miss him greatly.

As iron sharpens iron, so one person sharpens another.
—Solomon, Proverbs 27:17 (NIV)

One who has unreliable friends soon comes to ruin, but there is a friend who sticks closer than a brother.
—Solomon, Proverbs 18:24 (NIV)

Mentors Make the Difference

Mentors may also be friends, and their role in your life invariably pushes or challenges you in some way. Your first mentor may have been a sibling, parent, or grandparent. Maybe it was a teacher or coach, or perhaps a pastor or minister whom you looked to for advice.

An early mentor of mine was Coach Bill Moore at Bryan High School. Coach Moore was my geometry teacher. I was not much of a high school athlete, but Coach Moore helped me realize I enjoyed math. A year or so later, Mrs. Vick, my trigonometry teacher, took on the role of mentor in my academic life. She had also taught my mom, which made her one of my more "mature" teachers. Mrs. Vick was strict and did not waste time, and I respected her. It is highly likely that neither Coach Moore nor Mrs. Vick knew I considered them mentors, but their influence and a positive experience in their classrooms contributed to my becoming a math teacher.

If you don't have a mentor, consider asking someone you know and respect to serve in that capacity. Ask them to meet with you on a regular basis for one year. That could be as often as a weekly meeting over coffee or sharing a meal together once a month. Use this dedicated time for asking questions and listening as they reflect and share from experience.

> ### Recommended Reading
>
> If you would like to read an exceptional book about a mentoring relationship, check out *Tuesdays with Morrie* by Mitch Albom.

Kelly Davidson is the older brother of one of my

childhood friends, Kenny Davidson. (He's now the winningest football coach at Graham High School. Go Steers!) I saw Kelly as an older brother, and even in high school, he was a solid Christian leader. While I was a serving as a mission intern in Thailand, I was fortunate to have Kelly as a mentor. He delivered the news that my brother had been in a car accident and was in a coma. When I didn't know whether to stay in Thailand or return home, I can still hear Kelly's advice: "That's what family is for—to celebrate the good times and to provide comfort in the tough times. You need to be with your family." Kelly, thanks for the advice and thanks for serving as a mentor.

Once you have developed a trusting relationship, there will be times you need advice for a big decision. In addition to a parent, grandparent, former boss, or someone from church, a mentor is the ideal person from whom to seek wisdom and counsel. A mentor does not have to be older. Like my roommate Nez, a mentor can be a peer. Ideally, a mentor is someone you know well enough to pray with and someone who will provide feedback to make you better, even when the conversation is painful.

My wife is my closest friend and my best mentor. She has stuck with me through thick and thin. She has seen me at my best, as well as my worst—and she still loves me. And because she loves me, she is brutally honest, even when I don't think I need her honesty. Her insight inspires and pushes me to strive to be a better child of God, which may be the most important role a mentor can play. We all need someone like that in our lives.

DO YOU REMEMBER THAT ONE
SPECIAL HIGH SCHOOL TEACHER
OR A PROFESSOR YOU HAD
IN COLLEGE,
THE ONE WHO TAUGHT YOU HOW
TO THINK—NOT WHAT TO THINK—
THE ONE WHO PERSONIFIED
DISCERNMENT AND PROPRIETY
AND TREASURED THE PURSUIT OF
TRUTH NO MATTER WHERE IT LED?

—J.N. WHIDDON, *THE MENTOR*

Work the Process

My wife, Amy, and I have two sons, Will and Wes. A few years ago, the youngest, Wes, asked if I would talk with one of his close buds, Teddy (not his real name). Teddy was on staff at a small church in Colorado to work with the youth; however, his journey getting there had a few turns. After finishing high school, he started at a private Christian college where he had several friends. Like many college freshmen, he was not used to the freedom and lacked the discipline to study. As a result, his grades suffered. He returned home to work and save money while taking classes at a nearby community college.

After getting back on firm footing, he transferred out of state to another Christian university where he had several close friends whom he had met while working as a summer camp counselor. There he completed a degree in psychology with an idea that he might consider a career in counseling.

Upon graduation, Teddy was invited to interview with the church where he knew several families from camp. Having no immediate plans, he accepted the job, and he enjoyed working with the students and their families. During this time, he also dated a fellow counselor from camp, who was finishing her college degree. When they married, she commuted back and forth each day to work in a city about an hour away, and he began his second year at the church.

It was about this time when Teddy and I first spoke. He had started working on a seminary degree in theology, but I could tell he was not sold on it. When I asked him why he was getting another degree, he replied that it seemed like a good idea, if he was going to stay in ministry. He was, however, beginning to wonder if a job at a church was best for him, his marriage, and his future.

One of the first questions I asked Teddy was, "So what do you really want to do?" Teddy replied, "That's the problem. I don't know!" I assured him that he was not the exception; in fact, his response was normal. I shared that when I was his age, I went through several variations of the same feelings. I also told him that if he was willing to, at best, pursue his passion or, at the least, find a job that fit him better, then we had work to do—and it would not be a quick process.

"Then let's get started!" he responded, agreeing to look toward the future. He also agreed to keep his wife involved in the process when I explained that communication with one's spouse is essential when considering career changes and major life moves.

After several conversations, I asked Teddy to select five mentors, people who knew him well and who would provide candid feedback to the following questions:

- What are my strengths and positive qualities?
- What areas of improvement do I need to work on and grow?
- What jobs or type of work do you think I am best suited for?

I encouraged him to select individuals who not only knew him well but also had connections and might be able to make referrals for work. Since he was in church work, one of his mentors was a full-time preacher. As a result of this mentor's feedback, Teddy learned of an opening at a large church with a youth group larger than the one with which he had been working. He pursued connections and, eventually, he and his wife were brought in to interview. It was an outstanding opportunity and an increase in responsibility and pay, but he was unsure if he wanted to stay in church work.

Another mentor provided a contact which led to a sales position. After a series of interviews, he and his wife had another opportunity to consider. But they still were not convinced it was the right fit. After six months of staying in communication with his five mentors and trying to figure out what he wanted to do next, he learned of an opening in the Oklahoma Farm Bureau in a rural community, very similar to the small towns in which both he and his wife called home. The more they learned, the more they liked it, and the more he knew he was a fit. He was also convinced that he could succeed in this position. In addition, his wife discovered that several of her sorority sisters lived in the community, and one of them had a business in which she was a great fit.

They prayed about the opportunity, talked to their parents, and decided to make the move. Teddy worked hard in order to start strong and discovered that his personality was ideal for this position. After getting to know him better, I was not surprised when he informed me that he had one of the most successful rookie years ever. His wife hit the ground running, and the business she joined began to grow and excel as well. It was not an easy process, but

Teddy followed a proven plan, took his time, and benefitted because of it.

Too often we jump at the next opportunity for the wrong reasons:

- To get out of a job we don't like
- For an increase in salary only
- For a position that sounded right but turned out otherwise
- For a job we let someone else talk us into taking

If a job is worthwhile and is a good fit, then it is worth waiting to evaluate it thoroughly with research, referrals, a proper decision method, and prayer. It takes time and a discovery process to figure out what you really want to do. And it's okay if the career decision you make doesn't last a lifetime. We live in a constantly changing world, which means the question you ask may simply be, "What do I want to do *next*?"

Take your time and do your due diligence. The process works!

In summary, the steps of discovering your strengths, what you want to do next, and finding a job in that area are as follows:

- Identify five mentors who know you well.
- Ask them what they recognize as your strengths, areas to grow, and type of work that fits.
- Ask them to point you in the right direction for contacts and referrals.
- Begin researching potential jobs.
- Pursue those that fit you best.

The keys are discipline, sticking to this plan, and being patient. There is also a proven track record that another reason for success is including an accountability partner, which can be a current mentor, close friend, or spouse. However, everyone is busy, and I would recommend hiring a life coach, career consultant, or executive coach to walk with you through the process and ensure your desired outcome. Most often the result will be a job or line of work in which you are better suited than your current situation. But it can also include getting to know yourself better and identifying your strengths, areas in which to grow, enlisting the help of mentors, and perhaps even finding more than one opportunity to consider for future work.

More Questions to Consider

❑ What book will you read next?

❑ How will you make time daily to read?

❑ Who are your closest friends?

❑ Whom can you ask to be a mentor?

❑ Who is someone you can mentor?

7

WHAT'S YOUR PLAN?

Be brave enough to live the life of your dreams according to your vision and purpose instead of the expectations and opinions of others.

—Roy T. Bennett, *The Light in the Heart*

Once upon a time, tradition carved a clear path from the cradle to the grave. The mile markers for most middle-income and affluent Americans included a high school diploma, a college degree, and then a career. You committed to life as an accountant, banker, coach, doctor, engineer, fundraiser, lawyer, minister, nurse, or professor, and although you may have changed jobs, you never changed careers. Along the way, you dated, found your soulmate, married, bought a house, started a family, and worked your way through life. Then came retirement and a gold watch, which you no longer needed because you had nowhere to go.

Things have changed.

Thank goodness.

People today move across the country and back for work, love, and sometimes just for a change of scenery. Switching jobs is normal, and career changes are widely accepted. People telecommute, work from home, and work for themselves. "Company lifers," those who work at the same place until retirement, have become a rare breed.

How did we get here? Is it an insatiable desire to improve, grow, and "be all you can be" that drives us? Probably not. More likely, it's our unquenchable thirst for more. We've seen the entrepreneurial examples of those who have blazed new trails, such as Andrew Carnegie (steel), Henry Ford (automobiles and assembly lines), Sam Walton (discount stores), Steve Jobs (creative design), Bill Gates (computer technology), and Elon Musk (futuristic engineer). Their innovations along with advances in technology have opened doors that generations before us only dreamed about. We know that more, new, and different are not only possible, but are all within reach.

With So Many Options, Think Purpose First

Early on in this book, I asked you to consider what drives you—what your purpose on this earth is. Have you figured it out yet?

I'm sure you know some people who are driven by the accumulation of wealth. And sure, money matters, to a point. When you understand that you are uniquely designed by God, endowed with unique abilities, desires, and interests, money won't be your driving motivation. It can't be because you were made for more.

With that *more* in mind, what will you choose to pursue? What path will you take or carve for yourself? Yes, the traditional route is still there, but it is no longer the only option. High school graduates can choose from any number of alternate routes, including a gap year, community college, military, trade school, mission service, a combination of college and work, or going straight into the workforce. Mid-life, you may well decide to switch paths or bridge a few to create a new one altogether. The choice is yours, and as you choose, my encouragement is to ensure that you include God in your decision by evaluating your gifts and honoring Him by using them.

One method to use when planning your future, or even your next step, is to define your personal purpose statement and let it be a guide for your life. You may be familiar with the mission or vision statements for your church, school, or business. And I'm sure you recognize how taglines, mottos, or slogans help consumers understand and remember a company or organization's mission. Consider the following:

- Advocare—We Build Champions
- Disneyland—The Happiest Place on Earth
- Chick-fil-A—Eat Mor Chikin'
- Dunkin' Donuts—America Runs on Dunkin'
- Wheaties—Breakfast of Champions

Each one of these short phrases gives us an idea of what the company is about—its mission, purpose, or greatest desire. But what about a personal message, motto, or slogan that reminds you of *your* purpose and serves to motivate, inspire, and even challenge you daily to honor God in all you do?

My personal purpose statement is "Help Others Succeed." It's not perfect and could be taken negatively, but it works for me. I want to coach, encourage, and inspire clients, family members, and friends to become more successful. My purpose statement reminds me to put others above myself. I may revise this personal motto down the road, but for now, it serves me well in guiding my long-term goals and daily decisions.

A friend of mine shared with me that his personal purpose statement is "Seek Truth and Pass It On." This person has a passion for reading, instructing, and sharing knowledge, and is particularly passionate about sharing God's truth and other Christian wisdom. The statement guides his life and reminds him daily of what is most important.

What about you? What words best describe or sum up your driving desire? Do you have a slogan that reminds you to do your best and to be your best? If not, take some time now to think about it. You don't have to commit to this personal purpose statement for the rest of your life; it will change and improve as you do. The point of the exercise is to create a motto that fits your gifts, drives your behavior, and reminds you to honor God in all your decisions.

Use the following questions to help craft your personal purpose statement:

- What do you enjoy doing?
- What are you good at doing, perhaps above average?
- What would you like to be known for?
- What inspires and motivates you?
- What do you do well that honors God?

Your purpose statement is more than a motto or slogan; it's a tool to help you design a plan of action. You may eventually want to cast a long-range vision for your life, but let's not start there. Let's begin by drafting a plan for the next year or maybe the next two or three years.

> ### Remember
> If you have absolutely no idea what you want to do, you can make the decision a little simpler by eliminating what you know you don't want to do. Refer to back to Chapter 4 if you get stuck.

Planning with Purpose in Mind

Once you have selected a personal purpose statement, even if you know it's only temporary at this point, it can serve you well in the planning process. Use it as your decision-making filter when faced with choices, especially when it comes to planning your future.

If, for example, you work in the marketing, design, or creative space and are blessed with the ability to come up with interesting or insightful ideas, your personal purpose statement might possibly be, "To generate fresh ideas for clients." That purpose statement could then serve as the foundation for your answers to questions like those below to form a five-year plan.

Planning for the Next Five Years

Start by writing down the answers to the following questions:

- Where do you want to be in five years? Be as descriptive as possible.
- In order to get there, what goals do you need to set?
- If you want to accomplish those goals, what must be done in the next year to get started?
- To make progress in one year, what do you need to get started doing now?
- How will you honor God now and throughout the next five years?

One of the key components to creating that plan is considering where you want to be in five years. What do you want your day-to-day life to look like? With that destination in mind, you can then outline your plan to getting there just as you would set a course on your phone's route mapping app.

Don't Use God as an Excuse to Stall Out

I've noticed that when people can't seem to make a decision, they'll ask: "What does God want me to do?" We've already established the essential value of honoring God in our decisions, so I'm not saying that is a bad question. But don't make God an excuse to stall out. If you are asking what God wants you to do in an attempt to circumvent the decision-making process or to avoid making the wrong decision, you are using God as an excuse.

Stop it.

God has given you decision-making abilities and the capacity for higher-order thinking. It's this ability (and a few other things, like thumbs, and our inclination to wear clothes) that distinguishes humans from animals. Yes, next-step decisions can determine the direction of your life, so they are important. But they are not impossible.

The truth is, you can honor God in all you do, anywhere you study or work, at any stage in your life. Include God in all your decisions, ask Him to provide wisdom and discernment and to bless your decision. But He is leaving the final decision for you to make.

If you are unsure about your next step, don't worry. You are perfectly normal. Before forcing a decision or possibly making the wrong decision, take some time and enlist help. Once you've considered your options and mapped out a rough plan, ask trusted family members, friends, and mentors for input or advice.

There are many methods to create a life plan, so do a search and take a look at a few to find one you like that will help you look ahead and chart your course. I like the LifePlan process outline by Business Made Simple University, a Story Brand company developed by Donald Miller. LifePlan uses reverse-engineering, which is a "start with the end in mind" concept made popular by Stephen Covey. You start by writing your epitaph, then setting goals for where you'd like to be in ten years. Next, you list what you have to accomplish in five years in order to be halfway there, and finally, you list what must be done in the next year to work toward the five-year goals.

The bottom line is that you need a plan. Of course, you can follow the crowd, do what your friends are doing, do what you are expected to do, or simply take whatever opportunities come easiest without giving it much thought. But there's a good chance you might not be pursuing your passion, following your dreams, or honoring God. Take the time to define your dreams and identify your passions by crafting a personal purpose statement and then creating a plan with your purpose in mind.

The purposes of a person's heart are deep waters, but one who has insight draws them out.
—Solomon, Proverbs 20:5 (NIV)

The plans of the diligent lead to profit as surely as haste leads to poverty.
—Solomon, Proverbs 21:5 (NIV)

More Questions to Consider

❑ Have you drafted a personal purpose statement? If not, write it down.

❑ Does your purpose statement provide direction for daily and future decisions?

❑ Where is your five-year destination? Give it some thought and write it down.

❑ What do you need to do to move toward that destination?

❑ What do you need to do first? Let's get started!

DO YOU HAVE GRIT?

Nothing in the world is worth having or worth doing unless it means effort, pain, difficulty . . . I have never in my life envied a human being who led an easy life.

—Teddy Roosevelt

I made the decision to join the Corps of Cadets at Texas A&M University when I was seventeen, and I had no idea what I would have to endure during the next four years. Little did I know that I would grow in strength in many ways, one of which was a class set of push-ups. I was the Class of '82; therefore, I eventually built up strength to do eighty-two push-ups on command. Daily discipline and being prepared came as a result of having an inspection-ready uniform and dormitory room. And the mandatory requirement to be at my desk studying on weeknights from seven to ten provided a successful start to college academics. I committed early on to take whatever they threw at me, to endure the suffering, to persevere, and to use the experiences to develop character. I knew several men who had made it through the Corps alive—men like my father—whom I respected and looked up to as mentors. As far as I knew, everyone who entered the Corps survived the drills, so I hung on with hope. And that hope was a confidence that I would come out better for having endured.

Twenty-two of us started together as "fish" in Company F-2; only eight made it through to graduation. I'm proud to be one of the eight.

Unlike life in the Corps, the culture we live in seeks to make things more comfortable, easier, and less painful. Shortcuts and workarounds are standard operating procedure. No one wants to struggle, which is why so many people give up—on their health, their relationships, their education, their financial freedom. It seems easier to zone out with Netflix, call it quits, drop out, or just use a credit card.

It *seems* easier, but the cost is inevitably higher. Enduring through times of challenge and struggle and putting in the hard work is how we grow.

A while back, a friend saw me running one hot, steamy Saturday morning. At church the next day, he commented, "Are you nuts? Why are you running in this heat?" And you know what? His remark actually motivated me to *keep* running even though Texas summers are brutal. I don't run because I enjoy it at the time. In fact, when I'm running, there are plenty of times I am tempted to cut it short and go cool off. No, I run because I enjoy the aftereffects, benefits, and results. Running provides a good sweat that cleanses my body of impurities. The time pounding the pavement allows me to clear my mind and release stress. I feel a boost of confidence every time I complete a run—even when I end it completely exhausted. And to top it all off, running allows me to maintain at least a minimum level of health so I can enjoy playing with my grandkids and eating what I want (within reason, of course). Running is a means to an end—pain with a purpose.

In Romans, the Apostle Paul writes that "we glory in our sufferings, because we know that suffering produces perseverance; perseverance, character; and character, hope" (Romans 5:3–4, NIV). I don't know if I "glory" while running, but I know that my commitment to running has taught me perseverance. And I know that persevering in other areas of life has helped to (and continues to help) develop character.

A person of character is someone who has courage, honesty, integrity, loyalty, and a good reputation. People are not born with those qualities; they are developed by pressing through in spite of fear, by standing up for truth and what is right, and by keeping their word and fulfilling their commitments completely. Character is a result of perseverance or staying the course in spite of difficulties, obstacles, and discouragement. The end result of pressing on through the suffering and perseverance to develop character is hope. And hope is not wishful thinking but a confidence in the future.

Grit: The Missing Ingredient

That decision to endure, to stick to your word, and to fulfill a commitment is becoming more and more rare. America is the land of freedom, and one of those foundational freedoms is choice. The freedom of choice is a great thing! But as a society, we tend to use this liberty as an excuse to quit when the going gets tough. You're always free to change your mind, right?! When hard times hit or things don't go as planned, the world says, "Hey, life's too short for all that work! You deserve to be happy. Move on to something easier! Are you nuts? Why are you running in this heat?"

If you are a young adult and prone to giving up when challenges arise, I get it. When you've grown up in a culture where every member of every team receives a trophy (win or lose), why wouldn't you expect rewards to come with little or no effort? When you're allowed to quit the team or the band or anything else to "find a better fit" rather than being required to practice and persist, why *would* you hang in there? For the past few decades, parents have even shielded children from suffering everything from veggies to the consequences of bad decisions. Perhaps that was done out of love and with good intentions, but the end result is a generation that isn't prepared to fight through and press on when adversity hits. They—and maybe you—are lacking *grit*.

At the dealership where I bought my current truck, I was waiting while getting the oil changed. An acquaintance from church walked by the waiting room, our eyes met and

WHATEVER YOU DO, WORK AT IT WITH ALL YOUR HEART, AS WORKING FOR THE LORD.

—THE APOSTLE PAUL, COLOSSIANS 3:23 (NIV)

he started toward me. It was then I noticed he was wearing a nametag as a salesman. *What in the world?* I thought. *This guy is a successful geologist who works in the energy business. What's he doing selling cars?*

He must have seen my puzzled look because he quickly explained the cyclical nature of the oil and gas industry. He had been out of work as long as he could stand it. He and his wife had cut all unnecessary expenses, scaled back on their tastes, and had even begun using their savings.

His father had previously owned a dealership, so he grew up working in the car business, and he knew he could get a job selling cars. Working at the dealership was a natural shift for him, even though he was forced to start on the ground floor, but he was confident he could succeed due to his experience. His determination demonstrates grit in action from a seasoned veteran of the working world as well as a timely display of humility and willingness to do whatever it takes to rise to the challenge.

How do you respond to challenge? I ask because the way you handle adversity determines how you experience life and the success (or lack of success) you will achieve. If you can learn to respond well when things don't go your way, then your life will be more rewarding and fulfilling, perhaps even peaceful in spite of the storms.

The good news is it's never too late to develop grit. And you don't have to go through a crisis to build up your tenacity. Be proactive and take on a hard project, set a challenging goal and see it through, or make a commitment and complete it. You won't have to wait long or look far to find an opportunity to improve your grit. Difficult assignments are all around us and they will find you; just be willing to accept them. Here are a few examples of commitments that require persistence and consistent effort:

- Make your bed every day, take out the trash, do the dishes, help around the house.
- Take on a project at work that no one else wants because it is difficult.
- Sign up for a 5K run, start training, and get in shape.
- Sign up as a monthly mentor at a children's ministry helping underserved kids.
- Work weekly at a food pantry or homeless shelter feeding the poor.

"Work at It with All Your Heart"

Both of our boys found jobs right out of college. They were grateful to have steady work, but it was a grind, and my wife and I heard their complaints regularly. They, like so many people, learned early on that work can be the ideal setting to develop grit.

Your first job (or if you're like me, your second or third job) is *rarely* your dream job. After a few weeks or months, you wonder whether you should have taken more time in your search or perhaps used your parents' connections to land a better gig. You may even realize that you hate your work and dread going back.

Welcome to the club. A global poll by Gallup found that 85 percent of the world's workers don't like their jobs. That's a big club.

But just like most of life, you have control over the way you respond to your job. When you don't want to be there, it can be hard to get to work on time. It can also be tempting to call in sick, not because of illness but because you're sick of your job! The temptation to bail was great for both of our boys, but they each set a goal to make it one year. Having steady income, they realized, was a huge benefit. And once they got used to the way things operated in their workplaces, they knew what to expect and figured out how to deal with day-to-day hassles. In the meantime, they gave intentional thought to what they wanted to do next and what would allow them to use their God-given abilities and interests.

They each ended up making it past their one-year goals: one made it three years and the other two and a half. Sticking it out was not easy for either of them, but they hung in there, and they are better because of it.

Maybe you are in a similar situation at work. Here's the deal: You can see it as drudgery or a steppingstone. You can focus on everything you hate about your work, or you can set a goal to make it one full year in the job *and* have a good attitude in doing so. Remember, suffering builds perseverance, and perseverance builds character. My suggestion: Hold on to the hope that things can improve—that *you* can improve if you stick with it. Not forever. For one year. In the meantime, reevaluate where you are, where you want to be, and the next step to move you in the right direction.

You can do it *if* you fight off the urge to quit and ignore everyone who tells you to bail and find another job. Stick it out. Grow some grit. You will not regret it.

With one year of experience under your belt, you can begin the process of looking for the next job, perhaps something that is a better fit. But you also may discover that your current work has grown on you. Once you made the decision to stick it out, to have a good attitude, and to make the best of it, you may learn that you work with good people and realize that you are in a better environment than you first thought.

As I said in the previous chapter, it's fine to switch jobs or even careers. But if you bail out of every job when it gets irritating or boring, you may miss out on opportunities to grow personally and professionally.

Regardless of your age or how far along in your career you are, remember to weigh the pros as well as the cons anytime you're tempted to call it quits. Look for the advantages, like stability of income that enables you to pay off or stay out of debt or buy a home, or the consistency of living in a community where you can build relationships, be part of a local church, and grow a family.

If you aren't satisfied with your work at any point in your life (remember, 85 percent of the world isn't), revisit questions like, "What am I best suited for and what do I really want to do?" and "What is my calling?" And if you are nearing a benchmark of a certain number of years on the job, I urge you to consider your next goal, but please don't retire. Your best years are in front of you! You are filled with wisdom and experience. Take time to discover what you really want to do; find your calling. As you work through a new purpose statement and life plan, consider who you can mentor, where you can volunteer, and how you can help others. While you're at it, take on a challenge you might have put off for years. Do something hard and work on your grit!

> **I have told you these things, so that in me you may have peace.**
>
> **In this world you will have trouble. But take heart! I have overcome the world.**
>
> —Jesus, John 16:33 (NIV)

More Questions to Consider

- ❑ How do you respond when you face a crisis?
- ❑ Do you tend to quit or look for a way to endure?
- ❑ When is the last time you did something hard to build character?
- ❑ What can you take on that is not easy but will help someone in need?

9

WHAT WILL YOUR LEGACY BE?

> *Growth can be painful, change can be painful,*
> *but nothing is as painful as staying stuck*
> *somewhere you don't belong.*
>
> **—Charles H. Spurgeon**

It's not how you start; it's how you finish.

So let me ask you something: If you maintain your current trajectory, where will you end up in five, twenty, or fifty years? What will your finish line celebration look like?

I get that it can be difficult to look that far into the future, and I would be the last person to ask you to map out every day of your life between now and then. What I do hope this book encourages you to do is to consider how the things you do today, this week, this month, and this year all factor into who you become and the legacy you leave for those you love. Every step, every decision, every action moves us closer to or further away from that goal.

That's why I talk so much about being intentional about personal development and growth. For a Christian, the perfect role model is Jesus. His life and example can seem a little difficult to live up to, but Scripture does outline how Jesus grew from that baby in a manger into the Savior of the world. In his gospel, Luke writes, "And Jesus grew in wisdom and stature, and in favor with God and man" (Luke 2:52, NIV).

If we examine this verse we see a model for self-improvement in four essential areas:

- Wisdom (intelligence)
- Stature (physical health)
- Favor with God (spiritual relationship)
- Favor with man (interpersonal relationships)

Continuous improvement in these four areas, regardless of your age, allows you to develop into a well-rounded, maturing individual. More importantly, intentional, God-focused growth in each of these areas helps you become the person He intends for you to be so you can leave a legacy that points people toward Him.

Let's take a look at how we can be intentional with our intellectual, physical, spiritual, and interpersonal development.

Wisdom

One of the best approaches for learning is the Socratic Method. In a nutshell, this is a style of learning based on asking good questions and engaging in interactive dialogue that promotes critical thinking. The Greek philosopher Socrates inspired this model, and it is still used in education today, particularly in law school. In an article in *U.S. News and World Report*, law professor Lance J. Robinson explained why: "We still use this method today in law schools because it is often similar to cross-examination. By asking a series of questions meant to expose contradictions in students' ideas, they can be guided toward more solid conclusions while also learning how to find the flaws in someone else's thinking."

The Socratic Method is a good practice to use on your path to learning and wisdom. It's no coincidence that this book is full of questions! You can always learn by asking questions and then *listening* to others' input, to God's Word, and even to yourself.

While you're asking questions, you'll want to be discerning in what you take to heart. In Chapter 6, we discussed the value of books and other people as a means of gaining information and wisdom. If you don't consider yourself a reader of books and your main source of information is social media, I want to offer you a few words of caution. It is easy to slip into conversations on social media that turn mean-spirited and rude, and it can be tempting to say things online you would never say in person. Beyond that, the information you find in your feed, which has been curated to get you to engage and spend more time online, is likely to be overly opinionated and heavily slanted.

In response to recent and ongoing incidents in mainstream media in which less-than-accurate "news" has been shared, several of my friends and acquaintances have given up on mainstream media. They are choosing to use social media as their entire source of news. I understand their frustration, but there's a danger to this approach. Because social media presents information from and based on accounts you choose to follow, like, or connect with, you are, in essence, creating a personalized echo chamber. Put another way, this method is like living within a social media bubble; the only voices allowed in are from those with whom you agree. Maybe that is not always a bad thing, but it can make it difficult when you want to learn from a wider circle.

If you want real wisdom, get it from those who have years of experience. It will require actual face-to-face conversations that take time, but wisdom is a worthwhile investment.

The people who influence you the most are those with whom you spend time. That could be your parents, friends, co-workers, mentors, and pastors. You get to decide who is in that inner circle and whom you want to listen to and learn from.

Make learning and growing in wisdom a lifelong endeavor. Be selective about whom you are listening to and where you get your information. Then ask questions. Dive deeper. Compare what others say to what you read in Scripture and then decide for yourself what you believe.

The beginning of wisdom is this: Get wisdom, and whatever you get, get insight.
—Proverbs 4:7 (ESV)

Stature

Jesus grew in stature—physically. At some point in young adulthood, we all stop growing taller, but we should never stop taking care of our bodies.

The challenge here is to develop a lifestyle of healthy eating and exercise. The health of your physical body is foundational to growth in the other three areas. Without a healthy body, the other areas often suffer. Physical health and strength promote confidence; a healthy body fights off disease and allows emotional strength to withstand worry, stress, and even depression.

Your health also contributes to your quality of life. I know too many people who dismiss the thought that exercise and healthy eating are important. They're too busy or simply not interested. But take a look at this list of the leading causes of death in the U.S. from an article on *Medical News Today*: heart disease, cancer, unintentional injuries, respiratory disease, stroke, Alzheimer's, diabetes, influenza and pneumonia, kidney disease, and suicide.

Many of those ailments are preventable. While there are no guarantees that you can avoid cancer or Alzheimer's, you can reduce the risk and improve your odds of recovery by adopting a healthy diet and a regular exercise routine.

There are many sources to learn about healthy eating, but your common sense should tell you to avoid fast food, eat less, and reduce sweets. As far as exercise, research has proven that any workout raising your heart rate for thirty minutes at least three times a week is the baseline minimum. You only have one life to live on this earth and only one body to live in, so take care of it!

Do you not know that your bodies are temples of the Holy Spirit, who is in you, who you have received from God? You are not your own; you were bought at a price. Therefore honor God with your bodies.

—Apostle Paul, 1 Corinthians 6:19–20 (NIV)

Favor with God

To grow spiritually is to grow in your faith toward God. And faith is not a one-time event, such as saying a prayer to accept Jesus into your heart or getting baptized. Faith is a lifelong process of making daily decisions that affect the way you think, act, and believe. The following three choices will move you along in your faith journey:

- **Decide to be God's man.** This is the most important life decision you will ever make. Whether you are single or married, young or old, choose to be a child of your Heavenly Father. But that decision is only the beginning of a lifelong relationship.

- **Commit to growing in the Lord.** A good place to start is reading His Word daily. Reading Scripture is how we learn who God is and what is important to Him. The *One Year Bible* has worked well for me. Following its daily reading suggestions makes it easy to read the entire Bible in a year.

- **Pray daily.** Prayer is discipline that will help you grow spiritually. I keep a journal to record prayer requests and answered prayers, which allows me to reflect and see the results of the difference that prayer is making in my life. Find a friend to serve as an accountability partner or perhaps join a men's study group that encourages you to pray daily. Prayer is not just a good idea; I have found it a necessity.

Growing in faith is important at every stage of life. It's not something to put off until you reach a particular milestone. If you are single, unsure about marriage, or plan to stay single, do not think any less of yourself, and don't allow anyone else to belittle you, either. Develop a confidence that allows you to rise above foolish talk so that others are attracted to you by your spirit of love, joy, peace, patience, and kindness. Become a walking showcase of boldness, courage, and confidence by the way you speak and treat others so that people feel better having been with you.

If you are married, make the decision to be a godly husband. With more than fifty percent of marriages failing, if you want your marriage to be successful, then make the commitment to God that you will love your wife—His child and gift to you. Anything worthwhile takes time, effort, and energy, and a healthy marriage is no different. Take time daily to ask your wife about her day, then stop talking and listen. Don't think about your next question, just listen. Good communication is key to a strong marriage. If you have children, avoid prioritizing them before your marriage. They are important, but your wife will be there after the kids are gone, so don't neglect her. Most importantly, make time for one another. My wife and I began a practice of regular walks together, usually at least thirty minutes, which provide exercise, conversation, and a shared time of prayer. It's a practice that helps us grow closer to one another as we grow closer to God.

If you have children or plan to start a family, decide to be a godly father. Step up and be the spiritual leader of your family. That is not an easy task, but if you make it a priority and ask your wife to help, you can be successful. If you want your children to love the Lord, work at being a consistent example of a godly man. Let them see you reading your Bible daily and praying with your wife. It is also a great practice to eat dinner together as much as possible and get involved in a community of faith. You only get one chance to be a successful father, so make it count.

A saying we have framed at the house that serves as a great reminder:

> *A hundred years from now, it will not matter what my bank account was,*
>
> *the sort of house I lived in, or the kind of car I drove . . .*
>
> *but the world may be different because I was important in the life of a child.*

Favor with Man

Finally, relational growth with your fellow man is important. You may have heard of the self-made man, but I'm here to tell you that it's a myth. There is no such thing as a self-made man; we need other people! You need friends because life is hard, and you cannot make it alone.

Even if you consider yourself an introvert and prefer living or working alone, please don't isolate yourself. Make friendships that last, build relationships, and invest time in others. God made us as social beings; we are wired to be in community even if that community consists of only a few people at a time.

Two are better than one, because they have a good return for their labor;

If either of them falls down, one can help the other up.

But pity anyone who falls and has no one to help them up!

Though one may be overpowered, two can defend themselves.

A cord of three strands is not quickly broken.
—Solomon, Ecclesiastes 4:9–10, 12 (NIV)

Make Your Mark

A close friend of my wife's learned that her husband was having an affair. After a heated exchange, she stormed out of the house consumed with anger, got in the car, and began to drive. She thought of the mess her life was in and the damage this would cause their children, among other negative thoughts. She even entertained the idea of driving off an overpass to end it all. Fortunately, perhaps even by a Divine cause, the radio was on a Christian station. She heard the song "Legacy" by Nicole Nordeman and was convicted by the words, "I want to leave a legacy; how will they remember me?"

After listening to the entire song and reflecting on the good things in her life, then with support from family, friends, professional counseling, and God's help, the couple saved their marriage. In no way was it easy, but they made the commitment to grow *together*. Over time, her husband became a godly husband, father, and now grandfather. He stepped into the role of spiritual leader God designed him to be, which began with a renewed decision to be God's man. I have full confidence that their example of repentance, forgiveness, and trust in their Heavenly Father will be part of the positive and influential legacy they leave.

What will your legacy be? What do you want people to remember about you and say about you after you're gone? If you commit to a life of growing in wisdom, staying healthy, and honoring God in all you do, as well as making new friends and building relationships, there is a strong chance you will live an abundant life.

Decide to be a good example to others, to be a positive influence, to smile more and be friendly. If you can manage to do that, you will be remembered well.

LOVE THE LORD YOUR GOD WITH
ALL YOUR HEART AND WITH
ALL YOUR SOUL AND WITH ALL
YOUR STRENGTH.

THESE COMMANDMENTS THAT
I GIVE YOU TODAY
ARE TO BE ON YOUR HEARTS.
IMPRESS THEM
ON YOUR CHILDREN.

TALK ABOUT THEM WHEN YOU
SIT AT HOME AND WHEN YOU
WALK ALONG THE ROAD,
WHEN YOU LIE DOWN AND
WHEN YOU GET UP.

—MOSES, DEUTERONOMY 6:5–7 (NIV)

More Questions to Consider

❑ Do you feel stuck and stagnant, or are you growing, learning, and improving?

❑ Determine ways you can grow intellectually, health-wise, spiritually, and socially.

❑ Most importantly, will you decide to be God's man and grow your faith?

❑ Are you living in such a way as to leave a legacy?

10

WHAT MATTERS MOST?

Many people think they lack motivation when what they really lack is clarity. It is not always obvious when and where to take action. Some people spend their entire lives waiting for the time to be right to make an improvement.

—James Clear, Atomic Habits

Have you ever had a moment of clarity when you knew exactly what action to take? I have had several, all of which occurred after losing someone close to me. I cannot explain it other than to say that on more than one occasion, moments of great loss have also been times of complete clarity about my next steps.

I already shared that when I lost my brother Richard, I suddenly knew—beyond any doubt—that I wanted to teach math and coach. It didn't matter that becoming certified would take two more years of classes. *I knew* what I wanted to do, so I set the goal and pursued it, and I never second-guessed the decision.

Rich died about the same time the movie *Top Gun* was released. The emotion of Maverick losing his co-pilot, Goose, hit me hard. Do you remember the moment when Maverick freezes in fear during live combat? He clenches a set of dog tags in his fist and says, "Talk to me, Goose!" I have *felt* that moment. Since my brother's death, there have been many times that I've spoken similar words aloud, "Talk to me, Rich!" In those moments, I have found courage and strength in his memory and the bond we shared.

Several years after Rich passed away, I received word that my old college roommate, Nez, had died. The sobering moment was both shocking and revealing. Nez, "The Energizer," had seemed invincible. It was impossible to imagine that he had been killed. At the time of Nez's passing, I was dating a girl who wasn't "the one." I had met her folks, she had met mine, but we both knew our relationship wasn't going anywhere. After losing Nez, another moment of clarity gave me the courage to break things off with her.

Even more than Rich's or Nez's passing, an incredible woman inspired another one of my major decisions. JoAnn Nolen Walker was a devoted wife and mother. She loved to read, was a natural competitor (especially at the domino table and on the tennis court), and an outstanding child of God. She finished a degree in education but chose to stay home and raise her children for her first career. Her greatest desire was to teach them to love the Lord. She was an active volunteer at her church, teaching children's classes and ladies' classes and mentoring young mothers. When her own children no longer required her full-time attention, she completed a master's degree in adult education and taught in a women's prison.

I was lucky enough to call her "Mom."

Mom maintained a fit and healthy lifestyle and rarely visited a doctor, which might have even been a point of pride. When she turned seventy, her health also took a turn. She experienced dizzy spells and ran out of energy quickly. She also began fainting, something she had never been prone to before. It turns out she had a rare disease called Amyloidosis. By the time it was diagnosed, there was little that could be done to stop it from taking her life.

But you know what? Her confidence in her faith shone through brighter than ever. Mom had lived her entire life with her final destination in mind. Spending eternity in heaven and introducing people to Jesus were her driving motivations. She knew her purpose, had a plan, and pursued it with passion and love. When she realized her time on earth was short, I'm sure she was sad to say goodbye to family, but she was confident she would see us again. Her heart was fully aligned with Paul's writing:

> **I have fought the good fight, I have finished the race, I have kept the faith.**
>
> **Now there is in store for me the crown of righteousness, which the Lord, the righteous Judge, will award to me on that day—and not only to me, but also to all who have longed for his appearing.**
>
> **—The Apostle Paul, 2 Timothy 4:7–8 (NIV)**

When Mom passed, I was working at Texas Tech University. I had completed all required coursework on a PhD and was considering returning to Stephen F. Austin State University as Vice President for Development. It is common practice for doctorate students to complete their required coursework and then take another job to advance their career while completing their dissertation as the final step of earning their degree. There's also a risk of never finishing the dissertation; in fact, more than 50 percent of those completing the coursework never complete the dissertation. And without it, these students never receive a doctorate. In higher education circles, the doctoral students who fail to fully complete their degree are known as ABD, All But Dissertation. I didn't want to be an ABD, and I feared that moving on would slow my progress—or stall it completely. In my mind, failing to complete the degree was not an option.

Shortly after Mom passed away, SFA offered me the position. As I had before, I felt a sudden sense of clarity and peace; I knew it was the right time to move. And yes, I completed the dissertation and earned the doctorate.

A Great Cloud of Witnesses

In the book of Hebrews, the author refers to a long list of faith heroes from generations past—people who lived out their faith in God through obedience and perseverance—as a "cloud of witnesses." It is almost as if these Bible legends—Abraham, Joseph, Moses, Rahab, and so many others—are peering down from heaven, watching us run our race and are cheering us on, saying, "You've got this! You can do it! Just a little longer, hang in there!"

Rich, Nez, and Mom are in that crowd cheering for me and others they loved.

Who is in your "cloud of witnesses" cheering you on? Think of those who have served as a mentor, people you looked up to as examples of faith, those who provided encouragement when you needed a lift. Take a stroll down memory lane and recall moments with each of them. Imagine having a conversation with them. Perhaps when you need someone to call on in a crunch, they can still give you an extra boost of motivation, just like my brother does occasionally. *Talk to me, Rich!*

What Matters Most?

When your time on earth is over and you look down from heaven on those you have loved, will they include *you* in *their* cloud of witnesses? Are you making the kind of impact such that your example of grit, faith, and love will continue to provide strength to those you leave behind?

My hope for you is that you will choose today, and every day, to live in such a way that you make a difference by improving the lives of others—today and for eternity. When you are gone, I hope you will not only be missed but that you will also continue to provide inspiration for those who loved you.

SINCE WE ARE SURROUNDED BY SUCH A GREAT CLOUD OF WITNESSES, LET US THROW OFF EVERYTHING THAT HINDERS AND THE SIN THAT SO EASILY ENTANGLES. AND LET US RUN WITH PERSEVERANCE THE RACE MARKED OUT FOR US, FIXING OUR EYES ON JESUS.

—HEBREWS 12:1–2 (NIV)

More Questions to Consider

❑ Reflect on your life. What moments of clarity or major decision points have guided you?

❑ Who is in your cloud of witnesses, those who have gone before you but continue to inspire you?

❑ Are you living in such a way that your example will inspire others?

❑ Whom are you influencing? Whose life will your legacy continue to impact even after you've passed on?

CONCLUSION

*. . . choose for yourselves this day
whom you will serve . . .*

**But as for me and my household,
we will serve the Lord.**

—Joshua, Joshua 24:15 (NIV)

Living a life of meaning and purpose is not a one-time decision. It is a journey. There may be moments when you complete a task, fulfill a dream, or reach a goal, but I'm convinced none of us ever "arrive." There is always another hill to climb on this march from the cradle to the grave. But if you discover who you are and live into your purpose, the journey can be most enjoyable and rewarding.

It is easy to fall into the trap of living only to please yourself. It is the pattern and practice of the world in which we live. But I challenge you, don't fall into that pattern; rise above the temptation. Continue to grow, improve, and learn to become what God has designed you to be, while at the same time, living a life of helping, serving, and loving others.

A friend of my father's once shared sound advice that has stuck with me. He said there should be these three important things in any person's life:

- Someone to love
- Something to do
- Something to look forward to

Those three goals have served me well, and I answer them like this:

Loving someone else can help you live into your purpose and provide meaning to everything you do. I love my wife and want to live in a way that pleases her and provides for her. I also love my family and want to honor them in all I do. But bigger than both of those is living to please God. I know that He created me, gave his Son to live and die for me, and now continues to love me. I strive to make my life a daily response to live in such a way that shows my gratitude for His loving kindness.

The second goal of "something to do" has been the focus of this book. Some may think it does not matter what you do, but I hope you are now convinced that it matters a great deal. God has designed you uniquely, with abilities like no one else. We are also designed as creatures of choice. We can choose to ignore our calling and simply follow the crowd, or we can choose to find our purpose and live into it. Discover who you are, learn your strengths and weaknesses, find your purpose, and follow what God has impressed upon your heart. You will not regret it.

Something to look forward to can be both earthly and eternal. Ultimately, I hope everyone realizes we are created for so much more than only this life on earth. We each have a spirit, and God has placed eternity in our hearts. We can choose to ignore that longing, or we can live in such a way that eternity drives us. Something to look forward to can also provide incentive towards our life goals, work goals, family milestones, and other achievements.

If you discover who you are and why you are here, then it is much easier to find your purpose and follow your passions. May you discover that yours is a life worth living and may you be a blessing to others.

If you have enjoyed this material but may want or need help putting it into action, such as an accountability partner, the team at Walker Consulting Group can help. Please visit walkerconsulting.org for more information. We would like to see you succeed.

The fear of the Lord is the beginning of knowledge, but fools despise wisdom and instruction.
—Solomon, Proverbs 1:7 (NIV)

WHAT'S NEXT FOR YOU?

Whether you are looking for help as an individual, group, or organization, Walker Consulting would like to see you succeed.

- Contact us if are considering hiring a life or career coach.
- Let us help you start a small group or guys' group.
- Bring us in to launch a Men's Ministry.

There may be other ways we can help ensure you get the most from this book. Please visit the website, email, or call. We want to hear from you!

THE WALKER CONSULTING GROUP

walkerconsulting.org
info@walkerconsulting.org
936-585-3115

ACKNOWLEDGMENTS

More than two years ago, I committed to writing a weekly email, which I called Monday Message. Discovering that I found more enjoyment than frustration in writing, the idea of putting together a book developed. Several people had commented, "You should write a book," but it is thanks to my wife, Amy—her encouragement, inspiration, and regular reminders—that this book became a reality.

Jim Whiddon, a college classmate and close friend had written several books. His example served as an encouragement as did dialogue with regular readers of the Monday Message. Discussions with my friends Susan Duncan and Sarah McMurray also helped build the dream and desire of writing a book. I am grateful for their support.

I am also thankful for the mentors in my life. This list includes few of the people who have pushed me to ask myself tough questions: Bob "DB" Walker, my father and fellow fundraising coach; Larry D. Phillips, youth minister and drywall instructor; Bob "Tough and Flexible" Davidson, former missionary, AFC founder; Brian "Mad Dog" Miller, lifelong friend and fellow reader of good books; Larry "Legend" Henderson, mission leader in Thailand and skydiver.

Amy and I both come from families of faith and have been blessed with fathers who provided for and continue to support us. I am grateful to my dad, Bob Walker, and to my father-in-law, Burl McCoy. I can still see my mom reading her Bible every morning while drinking black coffee. I so appreciate JoAnn Walker for her example and my mother-in-law, Jan McCoy, who gave me my first One Year Bible that helped me become a daily reader of God's Word. My brother, Bill Walker and his wife, Shawna, as well as my sister, Rebecca Elkins and her husband, Charlie, are a source of continued family commitment. Marrying into a close-knit family has been a blessing, and I'm grateful for my brothers-in-law Brad McCoy and his wife, Debra, and Michael McCoy and his wife, Jan. May every reader strive to grow and develop strong families like those I have experienced.

BIBLIOGRAPHY

Asurion. "Americans Check Their Phones 96 Times a Day." *PR Newswire*, November 21, 2019. prnewswire.com/news-releases/ americans-check-their-phones-96-times-a-day-300962643.html.

Brueck, Hilary, and Shayanne Gal. "Suicide Rates Are Climbing in Young People from Ages 10 to 24. Here's How to Support the People You Love." *Business Insider Australia*, September 13, 2020. businessinsider.com.au/cdc-suicide-rate-in-young-people-10-24 -continues-climb-2020-9.

Camera, Lauren. "Across the Board, Scores Drop in Math and Reading for U.S. Students." *U.S. News & World Report*, October 30, 2019. usnews.com/news/education-news/articles/2019-10-30 /across-the-board-scores-drop-in-math-and-reading-for-us -students.

Castel, Alan. "Can Reading Help My Brain Grow and Prevent Dementia?" *Psychology Today*, April 11, 2018. psychologytoday. com/us/blog/metacognition-and-the-mind/201804/can-readin g-help-my-brain-grow-and-preventdementia#:~:text=Reading%2 -is%20a%20great%20way, time%20it%20also%20enhances%20 vocabulary.

Chiu, Allyson Chiu. "Americans Are the Unhappiest They've Ever Been, U.N. Report Finds. An 'Epidemic of Addictions' Could Be to Blame." *The Washington Post*, March 21, 2019. washingtonpost.com/ nation/2019/03/21/americans-are-unhappiest-theyve-ever-been -un-report-finds-an-epidemic-addictions-could-be-blame.

Clifton, Jim. "The World's Broken Workplace." Gallup, June 13, 2017. News.gallup.com/opinionchairman/212045/world-broken -workplace.aspx?g_source=position1&g_medium=related&g _campaign=tiles.

Dastagir, Alia E. "More and More Americans Are Dying by Suicide. What Are We Missing?" *USA Today*, January 30, 2020. usatoday.com/story/news/nation/2020/01/30/u-s-suicide-rate-rose-again-2018-how-can-suicide-prevention-save-lives/4616479002/.

Gladwell, Malcolm. *Outliers: The Story of Success.* New York: Little Brown and Company, 2008.

Kowarski, Ilana. "What Is the Socratic Method that Law Schools Use?" *U.S. News & World Report*, April 4, 2019. usnews.com/education/best-graduate-schools/top-law-schools/articles/2019-04-04/what-is-the-socratic-method-and-why-do-law-schools-use-it.

McKnight, Lori. "The 5 Gallup Insights You Need to Know." *CSI Stars* (blog), March 23, 2017. csistars.com/2017/03/23/5-gallup-insights-need-know/.

"Mental Health by the Numbers." National Alliance on Mental Illness, December 2020. nami.org/mhstats.

Nichols, Hannah. "What are the leading causes of death in the US?" *Medical News Today*, July 4, 2019. medicalnewstoday.com/articles/282929.

Perrin, Andrew. "Who Doesn't Read Books in America?" Pew Research Center, September 26, 2019. pewresearch.org/fact-tank/2019/09/26/who-doesnt-read-books-in-america/.

Sinicki, Adam. "The 'Adaptive Unconscious'—Is Your First Decision Your Best One? *Healthguidance.org*, January 25, 2020. healthguidance.org/entry/16989/1/the-adaptive-unconscious-is-your-first-decision-your-best-one.html.

Sullivan, Alice. "The Life-Long Benefits of Reading for Pleasure." *The School Librarian* 63, no. 1 (Spring 2015): 5–6. search.proquest.com/openview/9a60e7306dc0208ea98f0cdbf9a81f8a/1?pq-origsite=gscholar&cbl=296199.

Ward, Alex. "New Survey Shows Americans Are Unhappier Than They've Been in Years." *Vox*, March 21, 2019. vox.com/2019/3/21/18275796/happiness-report-usa-ranking-2019.

Wright, Jerold, Michael Sheridan, and Mark Dagostino. *Attitude: Develop a Winning Mindset On and Off the Court.* New York: Ballantine Books, 2017.

ABOUT THE AUTHOR

Sid Walker was born in Los Angeles while his father worked at Pepperdine University. The family moved to Texas when he was eight years old, and he has lived in the Lone Star State ever since, except one year in Bangkok.

Sid's work experience includes teaching math and coaching junior high, working at a fitness center, fundraising at the college level, private school administration, university administration, and now consulting. Through the late discovery of a love for reading, as well as learning from experience and mentors, his passion and motto for life is "Helping Others Succeed."

He and his wife, Amy, have two sons and three grandchildren.

Sid continues to believe that his best days are still in front of him.

Call or email, and let's get started!
sid@walkerconsulting.org
936-585-3115

Made in the USA
Las Vegas, NV
28 May 2022